A souvenir guide

Polesden Lacey

Surrey

CH00662335

Polesden Lacey: the nice a prudent distance of tov

4 Mrs Greville
6 An Edwardian powerhous

Polesden's Treasures 8

Tour of the House 10

11 Central Hall
12 Central stairs
13 Balcony
14 Mrs Greville's Apartment
16 Portico Bedroom
18 Dining Room
20 Picture Corridor
22 Library
24 Study
26 Saloon
28 Saloon collections
30 Tea Room
32 Billiard Room
34 Smoking Room
35 Gun Room

The Gardens 36

38 Tour of the Gardens
40 Admiral's Walk and
   Squirrel's Corner;
   Long Walk, Nun's Walk,
   Pinetum
42 Golf Course; Lawns;
   Front of the House
44 Sunken Gardens;
   Rockery; Croquet
46 Graham Stuart Thomas
   (1909–2003)
48 Herbaceous Borders;
   Winter Garden
50 Lavender and Iris
   Gardens; New
   Kitchen Garden
52 Cold Frame Yard
   and Potting Shed;
   Orchard
54 Rose Garden
56 The Ladies' Garden;
   The Pets' Cemetery

The Estate 58

59 Historic buildings
   and places

Servants 60

62 Stable Courtyard

National Trust

Polesden Lacey: the nicest place within a prudent distance of town

Polesden Lacey is just 25 miles from central London, yet its idyllic setting, nestled within the Surrey Hills, gives it a sense of seclusion and comfort that has seduced generations of visitors and owners.

An un-aristocratic estate

Polesden Lacey is not the long-standing seat of one aristocratic family. There has been a house on the site since the Middle Ages but no single family has owned the estate for more than a hundred years. Instead it has been occupied by, and often the passion of, a string of wealthy individuals.

From Anthony Rous to an admiral

The first substantial manor house was built for Anthony Rous in 1631. It remained in the Rous family until 1723, after which the estate passed through a series of owners and their families, all of whom added something to the house, gardens or parkland. The first of these was the Moore family.

Arthur Moore was an economist, politician and self-made man who owned nearby Fetcham Park. The Moores added an octagonal pavilion to the south front during their time here. Next was Frances Geary, a naval captain, who rose to the rank of admiral and spent his retirement at Polesden Lacey after purchasing it in 1747.

Writers, stationers and intellectuals

Playwright Richard Brinsley Sheridan came to live at Polesden in 1797. He adored the house and estate but his overly ambitious household improvements left it in ruins. In 1818, stationer and bookseller Joseph Bonsor bought Polesden and commissioned Thomas Cubitt to rebuild it in 1821–3.

Sir Walter Farquhar presided over Victorian Polesden but changed relatively little of Cubitt's building. Finally, in 1902, the estate was bought by Sir Clinton Dawkins, an ex-colonial civil servant and a member of The Souls – a loosely-knit social group made up of the most distinguished politicians and intellectuals of the day. He was also a business partner of J. P. Morgan. Dawkins commissioned the greater part of the building we see today from the architect Sir Ambrose Macdonald Poynter.

Mrs Greville

Super-rich socialite Mrs Greville was the last private owner to put her stamp on Polesden. She and her husband, the Honourable Ronald Greville, took possession of the estate in 1906. Maggie Greville, or 'Mrs Ronnie' as she was known, was a formidable hostess who made Polesden Lacey synonymous with leisure, indulgence and hospitality.

Background Polesden's east front

Mrs Greville

'Maggie Greville! I would sooner have an open sewer in my drawing room,' declared Lady Leslies. Cecil Beaton described Mrs Greville as a 'galumphing, greedy, snobbish old toad', while Prime Minister Arthur Balfour thought her conversation was 'a sort of honeyed poison'.

It is safe to say that not everyone was a fan of the self-proclaimed 'Beeress' Maggie Greville. However, there were clearly mixed feelings; author Osbert Sitwell recalled her 'innumerable acts of imaginative and creative kindness'.

Queen Elizabeth, the Queen Mother, may have summed her up best when she remembered her as 'so shrewd, so kind, so amusingly unkind, so sharp, such fun, so naughty…altogether a real person, a character, utterly Mrs Ronald Greville'.

'I'd rather be a beeress than a peeress'
Mrs Ronald Greville

Aspirations and influence

The illegitimate daughter of William McEwan, a millionaire Scottish brewer, and lodging-house keeper Helen Anderson, Maggie Greville was dynamic and ambitious. The young Maggie was part of a newly wealthy smart set, competing to entertain the Prince of Wales, later King Edward VII, in ever more lavish style. She used her father's wealth, her husband's connections and her own natural abilities to become one of the most influential hostesses of her generation.

In 1891, after marrying Ronald Greville, eldest son and heir of the 2nd Baron Greville, she embarked upon a career as a society hostess that would last for fifty years. Her guest lists from the period are a Who's Who of early 20th-century society, littered with royals, celebrities and politicians.

For most of her time at Polesden Lacey Maggie Greville was a widow. Her husband died in 1908 and her father in 1913, leaving her a woman of immense and independent fortune. She never remarried, remaining free to indulge in her favourite pastimes: travel, matchmaking and the pursuit of royalty.

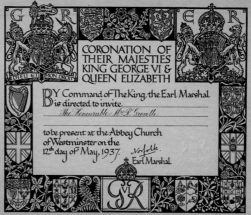

Above left Mrs Greville's invitation to a garden party during her tour of India in 1921

Above right The desk shows photographs of royalty known to and entertained by Mrs Greville

Left Mrs Greville's invitation to the 1937 coronation of King George VI and Queen Elizabeth

Opposite left Dated 1912, this photograph of Mrs Greville is by Lafayette and taken from a newspaper clipping

Opposite right Ronald Greville, Mrs Greville's husband

An Edwardian powerhouse

The house the Grevilles bought in 1906 was practically a new building. It incorporated only the southern façade and basements of the earlier regency villa by Thomas Cubitt.

Designed by Sir Ambrose Macdonald Poynter for Sir Clinton Dawkins between 1903 and 1905, Edwardian Polesden was a truly up-to-date country house. The mansion had electric power, en-suite bathrooms, stables, a 'motor house', outbuildings and all the many service rooms and conveniences needed to make it the height of modernity. With extensive gardens and a manageable estate of around four hundred hectares (one thousand acres) this was the perfect purchase for a glamorous society couple.

Putting on the Ritz

The Grevilles employed Mewès and Davis, the architects of the Ritz hotel, and pre-eminent interior decorating firm White, Allom & Co., to revamp the interiors of their new house. The principal reception rooms derived inspiration from a succession of different historical styles and made extensive use of architectural salvage.

Salvage was White Allom's speciality: gilded Italian panelling, an intricately carved 17th-century church reredos (an altarpiece, screen or decoration behind an altar in a church) and 18th-century marble fire surrounds were all employed to create appropriate settings for Mrs Greville's remarkable collection of art. The interiors became part of the collection and were designed to serve as a background to Mrs Greville's glittering parties. Upstairs Mewès and Davis showed off their own speciality – a series of elegant guest suites in the French style (see pages 14–16).

Politics among the plants

A typically English garden was created to impress the foreign ambassadors and dignitaries who came to Maggie Greville's house parties. Hothouses (heated greenhouses) and productive gardens supplied the enormously indulgent dining of the Edwardian elite. A nine-hole golf course and tennis courts completed this extravagant playground, offering sports that were both fashionable and sociable. Golf was a particular favourite of Mrs Greville.

The Eastern Approach

The exterior appearance of Ambrose Poynter's original yellow stucco villa was little changed by the Grevilles' architects. The most visible alterations were to the façade. Mewès and Davis extended the left-hand wing, adding to the principle apartments on the first floor and making room for a private study below. A matching bow front was also added to the right-hand kitchen wing.

Left Detail of a gilded cherub face and surrounding decoration, which appears on the Saloon door

Left Polesden Lacey as seen from Theatre Lawn

Below The Duke and Duchess of York playing golf during their honeymoon at Polesden Lacey (see pages 16–17)

The first royal visitor was welcomed to Polesden Lacey before alterations to the house were complete. In 1907 King Edward VII joined a day trip from the Grevilles' temporary residence, Reigate Priory. *The Onlooker* reported that 'his motor was not able to drive up to the house because the road way to the front door had not been built'.

Polesden's Treasures

Inside, Maggie Greville's house was – and still is – a treasure trove, containing typically Edwardian collections.

When, in 1942, Mrs Greville left Polesden Lacey to the National Trust 'for the largest number of people to have enjoyment thereof' she felt the main value of her bequest was in her collections. She anticipated that the National Trust might want to combine the contents of Charles Street, her London home, with that at Polesden Lacey 'to form a Picture and Art Gallery in a suitable part or parts of the house'.

'Full of rare china and expensive treasures'

Politician Sir Henry 'Chips' Cannon, 1939

During the Second World War James Lees-Milne, then Secretary of the Country House Committee for the National Trust, along with a host of experts, heavily 'pruned' the collection at Polesden Lacey. They left it with museum-quality treasures which included fine examples of Dutch, Italian and British paintings, Chinese and European ceramics, 17th- and 18th-century miniatures and silver as well as exquisite *objets d'art*.

Above This collection of boxes, now in a display case in the Saloon, would have held a variety of things including needle cases, a stamp wetter and a bookmark

Left A ceramic jar dating from 1660. It is now in the Picture Corridor

Left *The Alchemist* by David Teniers the Younger (17th century), which can be seen in the West Corridor

Below left and right *A Dutch Gentleman* and *A Dutch Lady* by Frans Hals, probably painted in the 1640s. The identities of these figures are unknown. The paintings can now be seen in the National Gallery of Scotland

My Pictures

A little notebook entitled 'My Pictures' records some of Maggie Greville's last notes on her paintings collection, including the auction houses from which she acquired them. Through her curling handwriting the world of a millionaire collector comes to life: a Reynolds from Agnew's, three Teniers from Lesser's, a Dutch Old Master or two from Christie's, an Italian predella from Sotheby's. The notebook also highlights the purchases made by her father, making plain the value she placed on his legacy. William McEwan had visited Chatsworth in 1850 and also travelled to Holland to look at paintings. His greatest interest was in Dutch art; his first purchases in 1885 were two paintings by Frans Hals, *A Dutch Lady* and *A Dutch Gentleman*, which he donated to the National Gallery of Scotland. Mrs Greville's donation of her collection to the National Trust in 1942 was in memory of her father, a continuation of his artistic philanthropy.

Left Mrs Greville's 'My Pictures' notebook

Tour of the House

From glittering golden walls to Maggie Greville's extensive collection of paintings and Fabergé objects, Polesden is a deliberately impressive house.

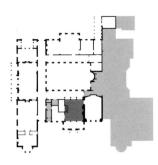

Central Hall

This Hall was part living room and part entrance hall functioning something like a hotel lounge. On a Saturday morning there would be the bustle of welcome as guests arrived for a house party.

In the evenings, author John Beverley Nichols remembered drinks being set out by footmen, before the guests went in to dinner. It was an informal room, with convenient access to the cloakroom and washroom.

Christmas brought an extra magic to the space as the double-height Hall was used for the annual servants' ball. A local newspaper article in 1911 reported that 'Mrs Greville personally opened the ball'. Later the grand hostess surprised the housekeeper's young daughter and her friend who were watching the dancing from the balcony. 'Why aren't you gels dancing?' asked Mrs Greville; the giggling girls didn't need a second invitation.

Woodwork

The wood carving which dominates the right-hand wall is a slightly irreverent addition to this Edwardian party house. Carved by Edward Pierce, it was made as a reredos for a Christopher Wren church, St Matthew's, Friday Street in the City of London (1682–5). White Allom & Co. installed the reredos, completely changing the feel of this space.

Above left A detail of the wood-carving from above the fireplace seen in the opposite photo

Above right A photo of the Hall as it was in 1926

Opposite The Central Hall

Central stairs
Balcony

Central stairs

Part of Mewès and Davis's work for Mrs Greville was to open up the landing of the sweeping central stairs. No doubt this was to increase its potential for making a dramatic entrance and to provide a view of Mrs Greville's portrait at the top of the stairs (see opposite page).

Ceramics

Mrs Greville briefly but enthusiastically collected Renaissance maiolica (tin-glazed earthenware), purchased for her by Finnish art historian, Tancred Borenius.

Designed for display and domestic use, maiolica was elevated to an art form by its *istoriato* – depictions of classical myths and legends. The most skilled painters of maiolica mastered perspective and used their limited range of colours to dramatic effect.

Seven of the twenty-three examples at Polesden Lacey are by Francesco Xanto Avelli, dating from *c.*1520–40. Avelli was keen to define himself as an artist. A poet as well as a painter, he started the trend of writing on the reverse of the dishes, describing the subject matter on the front. Other rarities in the collection include the three hawks or parrots from Urbino, dating from *c.*1570.

Right A ceramic parrot from the Italian (Urbino) school, dating from 1560–1600 and an Italian maiolica *tazza* (shallow, saucer-like dish mounted on either a stem and foot or just a foot) by Francesco Xanto Avelli

Above Central stairs in 1905

Opposite top H.H. The Maharaja of Mysore with Mrs Greville in the Rose Garden at Polesden

Opposite A group of pre-eminent figures, including King Fuad I, the King of Egypt and Mrs Greville

Balcony

The visitors' book records decades of house parties, liberally studded with royalty. King Edward VII visited in 1909; King George V and Queen Mary in 1914. In 1923, the Duke and Duchess of York honeymooned here (see pages 16–17) and were regular visitors before and after the Duke's ascension to the throne as George VI. The King of Egypt, the Queen of Spain, Aga Khan III and the Maharaja of Mysore all enjoyed the comforts of Polesden Lacey.

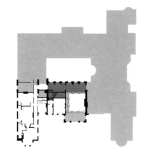

Keeping up with the fast set

Part of the racy Marlborough House Set, Maggie and Ronnie bought Polesden Lacey to host Saturday-to-Monday house parties. High Society's rules were looser at these house parties. Mrs Greville stated that she 'never follow[ed] people into their bedrooms; it's what they do outside them that counts' – a pragmatic attitude for a hostess who was expected to allocate bedrooms which discreetly facilitated the latest liaisons. Alice and George Keppel in particular were close friends of the Grevilles and appear regularly in the visitors' book. Alice became King Edward VII's mistress in 1898. Known as 'La Favorita', she was essential for the success of any party where the King was a guest.

Margaret Anderson, the Honorable Mrs Greville DBE (1863–1942)
Painted the year she married, this virtuoso portrait shows Maggie Greville at the height of her career. The painter – Carolus-Duran (1837–1917) – taught his students, including John Singer Sargent, how to paint *au premier coup* (wet on wet), stroke by stroke without reworking. The progressive technique gave his work a dynamic and instantaneous look, concentrating on form, colour and light. Unlike Carolus-Duran's portrait of Daisy, Countess of Warwick, another member of the Marlborough House set, this painting was never exhibited publicly; the sensation was for Mrs Greville's guests only.

Mrs Greville's Apartment

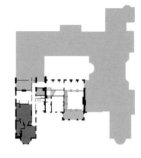

Mrs Greville's private apartment consists of a master bedroom, boudoir and bathroom, with a maid's room and bathroom opposite.

A 1917 Otis lift provided access down to the private courtyard entrance and ground floor Study. The adjoining Chippendale Bedroom was probably originally intended for Ronnie Greville, who died in 1908.

In 1910, *The Onlooker* reported that 'the corridor serves as a sort of picture gallery for the portraits of its mistress's more intimate personal friends. The last royal group was taken in the colonnade only a year ago on the occasion of King Edward VII's visit last year.'

'She told me one day that during the morning three kings had been sitting on her bed'

Kenneth Clark, Art Historian, in *Another Part of the Wood: A Self-Portrait* (1975)

Left The lavish Bathroom, with its marble-tiled walls and silver-plated basin legs, is a rare survival. It is very similar to those installed by Mewès and Davis at the Ritz, since destroyed

Right Plasterwork ceiling detail

Royal relationships

Mrs Greville was very keen to make herself relevant to a younger generation of royals. Great friends with Queen Mary, Maggie also sought the acquaintance of Edward, Prince of Wales, following him around India on his 1922 tour. The Prince preferred a younger set and Mrs Greville never succeeded in gaining his friendship; instead her most enduring royal relationship was with King George V's second son, the Duke of York, later King George VI and his bride, Lady Elizabeth Bowes-Lyon.

'I was so happy in the days when they used to run in and out of my house as if they were my own children,' remarked Mrs Greville to Harold Nicholson after the Duke and Duchess became King George VI and Queen Elizabeth. Polesden Lacey was a special place for the royal couple and Mrs Greville agreed with George V in 1914 that 'Bertie' would inherit the house. It was only in 1942, after Mrs Greville died, that the royal family discovered it had been left to the National Trust. Queen Elizabeth, who inherited Mrs Greville's fabulous collection of jewellery, took the news about the house well, writing to her husband, 'I'm not sure that this isn't a very good idea because it is a very difficult place to keep up'.

The Archduchess

In her will Mrs Greville requested that her 'valued friend Marie Adeline Liron' be given tenancy of the apartment for life. Nicknamed the 'Archduchess' by Mrs Greville because of her dignity and natural distinction, Mademoiselle Liron was Mrs Greville's personal maid. As the bequest shows, she was as much a friend as a maid. The apartment was first opened to the public in 2011. Many of the furnishings were sold or loaned out after Mrs Greville's death, but the fabulous ceilings and the decadent bathroom suite remain.

Ceilings

In her own apartment Maggie chose a fusion of styles from Mewès and Davis's repertoire. The Boudoir ceiling is a copy of a Jacobean ceiling from the Reindeer Inn, Banbury. The panelled walls were originally unpainted oak, and were only painted after a fire in 1960. The Bedroom took inspiration from the 18th-century designs of Robert Adam, but was furnished in the Chinoiserie style.

Above Adeline Liron, Mrs Greville's personal maid and companion

Right An archive photograph of Mrs Greville's bedroom

Portico Bedroom

Polesden Lacey's guest bedrooms were comfortable and modern; many had telephone connections and en-suite bathrooms.

Below Portico Bedroom

For a couple staying at Polesden on their own, the Portico Bedroom is appealing, located as it is, close to the Dining Room and principal entertaining spaces. It is now thought that this was the room given to the Duke and Duchess of York on their honeymoon in 1923, rather than King Edward VII's royal suite on the south front.

The décor

An inventory taken in 1943 records the Portico Bedroom being furnished with a bedstead 'painted with festoons of flowers on green and gold with an embroidered silk canopy'. The present gilt walnut bedstead came from the Copper Beech Bedroom. The room is furnished with much of what remains of the furniture from Polesden's other guest bedrooms.

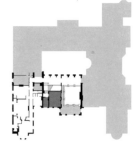

Portico Bathroom

Polesden Lacey had 15 guest bedrooms, nine of which were en-suite. In the early 1900s even the grandest houses usually required guests to share one bathroom between three bedrooms. The Portico Bathroom has several interesting features of Edwardian plumbing. The heated towel rail on the left wall is very much an Edwardian invention and the tap-less bath, which fills from a silver disk at the base of the bath, is the height of sophistication. It avoids the 'small geyser of rust-coloured water...which was in any case stone cold' described by one contemporary as characteristic of early bath-time experiences.

The Queen Mother had a fondness for the Portico Bathroom, asking to revisit it during her tour in 1970. The Duke and Duchess also returned to Polesden Lacey to celebrate their 9th wedding anniversary.

The royal honeymoon

The Duke and Duchess of York had the house to themselves. Official photos show them enjoying golf and relaxing on the South Terrace. 'This is a *delicious* house, & the food is too marvellous,' wrote Elizabeth, Duchess of York on the first day of her honeymoon.

Media coverage was extensive; a light aircraft even flew over the house in attempts to get photographs. The *Illustrated London News* produced a double-page spread on 'The Honeymoon House'. For society hostess Mrs Greville, a royal honeymoon was the ultimate triumph.

Above left The Portico Bathroom

Above right The Duke and Duchess of York (later King George VI and Queen Elizabeth) on their honeymoon

Left This painting, *Eva Maria ('Violette') Veigel, Mrs David Garrick (1724–1822) with a Mask*, attributed to Johann Zoffany, 1733–1810, can be seen in the Honeymoon Suite

Even the formidable Mrs Greville might be forgiven for having a tremor in her heart at her first dinner party in this Dining Room. She had been widowed just a year and this was the occasion she and Ronnie had planned to launch their new house and to entertain King Edward VII. Today you can see a recreation of that meal in this room; it is displayed as it would have been on Sunday 6 June, 1909.

'The first dinner party causes a tremor to the stoutest heart. No really first class entertaining can be done where money is an object. It is not necessary to be ostentatious or lavish, but all perfection must be paid for and requires a great deal of care and forethought.'

Lady Violet Greville (Mrs Greville's mother-in-law), *The Gentlewoman in Society*

Above A view of the Dining Room, with the table set for the final course (the *extremet*), which then would have been a mixture of sweet and savoury foods

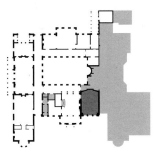

The meal was relatively light by Edwardian standards with just six courses.

The dining-table is not original to the room but represents the long linen-covered table Mrs Greville favoured until the 1930s. In 1933 her conversion to a new round lacquer table, with a glass-covered lace top was apparently newsworthy and reported in the society pages of the *Daily Telegraph*.

Above right *The Paterson Children* by Henry Raeburn, *c.*1789/1790. This oil painting depicts Margaret, John and 12-year-old George, the children of George and Anne Paterson of Castle Huntly, Perthshire

Paintings

Hung around the damask walls are Mrs Greville's famous portraits, works by Henry Raeburn (picture numbers 6, 7, 8 and 10), Thomas Lawrence (11) and Joshua Reynolds (9), and from the studio of Peter Lely (3). Writer John Beverley Nichols remembered Winston Churchill at Polesden in 1930, holding forth after dinner about the German Menace 'with a good cigar in one hand and a better Armagnac in the other…behind him…one of Raeburn's finest pictures, the Paterson Children'. Mrs Greville followed her father in collecting works by the Scottish artist. *The Paterson Children* (7) *c.*1790 was the most expensive painting she ever bought, costing £23,000 in 1918.

On the west wall is a more personal work, a portrait of Mrs Greville's father, William McEwan, by Benjamin Constant. Mrs Greville recorded that it was a 'striking likeness' painted 'hurriedly' in six sittings at the Savoy Hotel.

Food and service

In the north-east corner of the room is the jib door. It was from here that the butlers and footmen would serve. Culinary standards were high; the food at Polesden Lacey was described as 'unsurpassed anywhere' by the *Daily Telegraph* in 1930. The chef for the royal visit in 1909 was probably a Frenchman, Monsieur Delachume; later Mrs Greville employed several female cooks.

'Like Jazz night at the Palladium…'

Considering Mrs Greville's high standards, her favourite male servants enjoyed a surprising amount of leniency. Writer Sir Francis Osbert Sitwell, 5th Baronet, described one particularly lively evening: 'I came back from Polesden yesterday night. It was like jazz night at the Palladium. All the butlers were drunk – since Maggie was ill – bobbing up every minute during dinner to offer the Duchess of York whisky.'

Picture Corridor

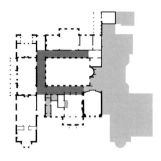

The Picture Corridor makes up three sides of the Inner Courtyard. The main route to the formal rooms in the house, it also acted as a picture gallery.

The ceiling was made by George Jackson and Son in 1906 and is a copy of a Jacobean original in the Long Gallery at Chastleton House in Oxfordshire (also National Trust). The walls are now hung with some of the best paintings in Mrs Greville's collection, many of which were originally displayed in her London home.

Collecting influences

Maggie Greville was not known among her acquaintances as a woman of great artistic knowledge. Beverley Nichols wrote that 'her taste in pictures was by no means impeccable'. She was considered too ostentatious and too rich to be a connoisseur. Yet she acquired a first rate collection.

Certainly her collections were influenced by her father's purchases, her Scottish ancestry, her art dealers and friends and by her relationship with the royal family. Her

Below left *A Village Inn* by Isack van Ostade, c.1641–1649. This oil painting depicts a group of peasants gathered with horses outside the eponymous village inn

Below right *The Artist as Virtuoso at his Easel* by Frans van Mieris (1635–1681), a self-portrait of the artist at 32. Van Mieris was second only to Rembrandt in the number and variety of self-portraits he made

acquisitions are a snapshot of the tastes of her social set, responsive to the advice of professional dealers and art historians of the day, but with her own tastes playing a part.

The collections

The core of the collection consists of 13 Dutch Old Masters known to have been collected by William McEwan, including *The Golf Players* by Pieter de Hooch (picture number 44) *c.*1660 and Gerard ter Borch's *An Officer Making his Bow to a Lady* (50) *c.*1662.

Mrs Greville's first purchase of an Old Master painting was *A Venetian Gentleman* by the Italian Bernardo Strozzi (47) through art dealer Horace Buttery for £650. In 1919 and 1920 she bought nine 17th-century Dutch portraits from two London art dealers, Agnew's and Colnaghi, including the exquisite and meticulously painted self-portrait by Frans van Mieris (60).

Tancred Borenius, a Finnish art historian and professor at the University of London,

one of a new breed of 'consulting art historians', advised Mrs Greville, particularly on her Italian acquisitions. With his help in the 1930s she bought the predella panel attributed to Perugino, *c.*1475, *The Miracle of the Founding of Santa Maria Maggiore* (20).

Borenius also assisted Mrs Greville with her collection of works by the French artist Corneille de Lyon (active 1533–74). Born in The Hague, Corneille was naturalised as French in 1547 and was painter to two kings of France, Henry II and Charles IX. Among his works owned by Mrs Greville is a portrait of King James V of Scotland (15) and one of Catherine de' Medici (17).

> 'She was very fond of pictures and objects of art'
>
> Osbert Sitwell, in Mrs Greville's obituary published in *The Times*, 17 September 1942

Images below clockwise from left

The middle-aged Queen Catherine de' Medici by Corneille de Lyon, *c.*1536

This painting by Elisabeth Louise Vigée Le Brun, dating from some time after 1773, is supposedly of her brother but we now are not sure this was the case. We think instead that it is essentially a subject-picture

This oil painting by Jacob van Ruisdael, dated 1677–1682, depicts the Zeider Zee coast in the Netherlands. Muiden and Mindensberg can be seen in the distance

Shipping in a Calm from the studio of William van der Velde the younger, *c.*1666

Library

In 1933 the *Daily Telegraph* declared the Library 'the apartment most used by the hostess and the many distinguished guests who come to stay with her'. It is easy to see why; the room, which remains much as it was then, is the most welcoming of the reception rooms.

The warm cream walls and golden carpet are offset by the blue and white of the Chinese Kangxi porcelain (produced 1662–1722). The design, by Mewès and Davis, was inspired by the work of 18th-century French architect, Louis-Rémy de la Fosse.

The books here are an amalgamation of libraries: some are from the Polesden Lacey and Charles Street libraries; other volumes belonged to the servants' social club, once located in the stable courtyard. The 1933 article stated 'there are discreet little notices in front [of the bookshelves] saying: Please do not remove books from this library, and when read, kindly replace'.

Photographs

The *Daily Telegraph* article also noted that 'photographs abound, notable ones being of the Aga Khan, Sir John Simon, the late Lord Balfour, and Sir Robert Horne all with signed inscriptions testifying to their friendship for this popular hostess'. Many of these can still be seen today on the two desks in this room.

Displayed on the Carlton House desk by the window is a photograph showing Mrs

Top A view of the Library

Above Mrs Greville in Hollywood with Wendy Barrie and Spencer Tracy

Right Framed photographs, a telephone and calendar on the writing-table in the Library

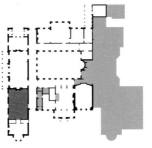

Greville in Hollywood in the 1930s. She is posing with actor Spencer Tracy and actress Wendy Barrie. Maggie Greville was an inveterate traveller visiting India, Australia, New Zealand, South America, Singapore, Egypt and Burma as well as taking frequent European trips. Sir Bruce Lockhart wrote that 'her vanity is inordinate. In those countries where she is not given a special train, the local British ambassador or minister gets sacked'.

Miniatures and paintings

On the table are two cases of miniatures. Mrs Greville collected these between 1891 and 1910 and they date from the 17th to the early 19th century. They include works by Peter Cross (c.1645–1724) (item number 12), miniature painter to the King, and John Smart (1742–1811) (36, 37), who painted portraits for the East India Company.

Above the fireplace hangs *One-year-old Boy with a Sheep* (1639) of uncertain attribution. Traditionally thought to have been by the Dutch artist Aelbert Cuyp, better known for his golden landscapes (No. 36 in the Picture Corridor, for example), it may in fact be by Caesar van Everdingen (c.1606–1678).

The smaller paintings flanking the fireplace and the self-portrait on the table are all by Scottish artist George Manson, a favourite of William McEwan. They date from 1869–74.

The furniture

The furniture is a blend of English, French and Italian dating from the 17th and 18th century. The upholstered chairs are covered with *gros point* needlework (embroidery done with large stitches).

Right above **Miniature portraits in a display case**

Right **A close-up detail of the top of the small 18th-century cabinet in the** Library. This cabinet was of particular importance to Mrs Greville. It was a gift from her great friend Queen Victoria Eugénie of Spain in 1920

Study

This is Maggie Greville's private study, a room where she spent much of her time. Self-contained, it has its own washroom, access to the lift from her apartment upstairs and a private entrance into the courtyard. The view from the main window takes in Bagden Drive, the original entrance to the estate.

An ingenious window

The window arrangement allows both a window and a fireplace in the centre of the south wall. The chimney flu bends to the left, running behind false books in the bookcase. The window, which looks out across the valley, was covered in the evening by mirrored shutters, creating a more intimate setting for the exchange of confidences.

Dangerous politics

Mrs Greville was a political hostess; she was also a dedicated correspondent, writing to countless ambassadors and politicians from her desk in this room. Her penchant for exerting her political influence led her into dangerous territory in the 1930s. Through her friendship with Joachim von Ribbentrop she was invited to a Nuremburg rally in 1934 and, being Mrs Greville, managed to obtain a private audience with Hitler.

Above **A view of the Study**

'She sat back in a large chair, like a Phoenician goddess, while the cabinet minister or ambassador leant forward attentively.'

Kenneth Clark, *Another Part of the Wood: A Self-Portrait* (1975)

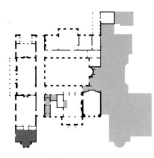

She had also entertained the fascist Count Grandi, Italian ambassador to London 1932–1939, and was quoted at the time as being 'enthusiastic' for the brown shirts (Barbara Cartland, *Search for Rainbows*). In Harold Nicholson's opinion she was a 'silly, selfish hostess' who dangerously conveyed the impression that 'foreign policy was decided in [her] drawing-room'. She was firmly in the appeasement camp in the lead up to war.

Mrs Greville's guest list for New Year 1936–7 shows the range of her social and political acquaintances and raises fascinating possibilities regarding the conversations perhaps held within these walls. Guests at that festive house party included: the American Ambassador, the Deputy Under-Secretary of Foreign Affairs, the Belgian Ambassador, Nazi party member Otto von Bismark and his wife Ann-Mari, and Sir Austen Chamberlain, half-brother to the prime minister and at that point a supporter of Winston Churchill's anti-appeasement stance. There must have been many considerations for the hostess as she allocated rooms and made her table plans for dinner.

Viscount Simon described one interaction when Mrs Greville 'took Ribbentrop to task, with her usual directness, by calling attention to the language of his invitation card. The Ambassador haughtily justified his innovation by claiming that the Germans, in view of their position in the world, were entitled to send

out such invitations in their own tongue. "Well", said Mrs Ronnie, "it would be very awkward if the Siamese took the same course".' Mrs Greville reversed her pro-Nazi opinions on the outbreak of war and, with typical flair, bought a Spitfire for the nation.

Ceramics

The glass cabinets on the left hand side of the room display 18th-century Meissen and Furstenberg porcelain, including this rare tea and coffee service, c.1770 decorated with singeries (monkeys pursuing human activities) (item number 79).

Above Mrs Greville at a Nuremberg rally in 1934

Below Dating from 1770, this porcelain German milk jug and teacup are by C. G. Albert and feature monkeys dressed as humans. They were painted and gilded by hand

Saloon

Left A view of the Saloon, in which the portrait of Mrs Greville can be seen in situ

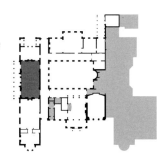

'A room fit to entertain Maharajahs in'

This was the apparent request from Mrs Greville to her architect Arthur Davis according to his daughter, Mrs Thomas Davis. The Saloon was the result and, with its glittering Baccarat chandelier and gilded Italian panelling, it certainly lives up to the brief. The panelling was probably supplied by White Allom & Co., taken from an Italian *palazzo*, c.1700. Sadly the fabric elements of the room were destroyed by fire in 1960 and the room had to be regilded and painted.

The Saloon was clearly designed to impress but not everyone was a fan. Beverley Nichols described it as 'really quite appalling – over-gilt, over-velveted, over-mirrored like an extremely expensive *bordel* [brothel]'.

Royally entertained

The room functioned as the large drawing-room and evening entertaining space during weekend house parties. Mrs Greville would often invite acts from London to come and entertain her guests. During the weekend of 27–29 July 1929, for the visit of King Fuad of Egypt, Mrs Greville pulled out all the stops. Chauffeur Frederick Hart was sent to Brighton to pick up the Dolly Sisters, music hall stars, and the gossip columns reported that during that same weekend 'entertainment was given in the saloon comprising of dancing and juggling in the Eastern tradition'.

Left This brooch features a green enamel ground and the cypher of King Edward VII in diamonds surmounted by a crown. It was produced by Collingwood & Co, who were jewellers to the royal family

Above The Dolly Sisters, who entertained Mrs Greville's guests in the Saloon, had toured the dance halls and theatres of Europe, including the Moulin Rouge, with their glamorous dance act

Saloon collections

Today, the best of Mrs Greville's French furniture is displayed here along with her collections of oriental ceramics, Meissen figurines and *objets d'art*.

The furniture

A bombe commode stands in the centre of the wall opposite the window. It is made out of kingwood with inlaid marquetry and gilt metal (ormolu) mounts. It dates from c.1750 and is by cabinetmaker Jacques-Philippe Carel. The ormolu is said to be signed by Jacques Caffieri, one of the most famous Rococo bronze sculptors. Caffieri was founder and chaser to King Louis XV. On the window wall to the right is a marquetry (decorative veneer) commode with Chinoiserie (Chinese-influenced) scenes, likely to be by the German Parisian ébéniste Christophe Wolff. Around the room there is a set of six giltwood armchairs from c.1760.

Images below left to right

The Japanese-made 1720 porcelain insect cage from H.M. Queen Mary

A Meissen ceramic scent bottle from c.1765. It was made by Meissen Porcelain Factory, which remains a luxury brand today

A late Ming (17th-century) stoneware pillow in the form of a tiger

A Carl Fabergé bookmark. The underside features a gold mark of a woman's head, denoting that the object was made after the end of the Tsarist regime

Fabergé

Mrs Greville, like the royal family and the rest of Edwardian society, was captivated by the work of Russian jeweller Carl Fabergé; there are a number of pieces by Fabergé in her collection (item numbers 14, 16, 47, 49e, 49g, 49h, 49i, 72, 73). Fabergé established a London shop in 1903 and sold over 10,000 objects between 1903 and 1915. His success was assured by the patronage of the royal family.

Small precious objects were important social currency in Edwardian high society. We know that Mrs Greville purchased at least two gifts for the royal family from Fabergé: a scent bottle in 1909 for £11 5s and a model of Edward VII's dog, Caesar, for £35 (now in the Royal Collection). The royals often gave Fabergé objects in return but also patronised other jewellers. For example, the jeweller Collingwood & Co., a more traditional jeweller, made two brooches and a seal for Edward VII who presented them to Mrs Greville (22, 23, 25).

Oriental ceramics

Mrs Greville shared with Queen Mary a love of oriental jade and ceramics. In one of the cabinets is a ceramic insect cage c.1720. It was made in the Japanese town of Arita and given to Mrs Greville by Queen Mary in 1920. The accompanying note suggests, 'this may amuse you'. The cabinets around the room display a great variety of porcelain, from devotional statues to a light-holder in the shape of a cat and a ceramic pillow. Most of the ceramics are from the reigns of the Chinese Emperors Kangxi and Qianlong in the 17th and 18th centuries.

The ceiling

In the border of the ceiling and above the doors are inset canvases of putti holding garlands of flowers. The roundels (circular emblems used as symbols) in the four corners show incidents from the life of David in the Old Testament. The paintings were damaged by the 1960 fire but it is suggested that they are by the Neopolitan, Paolo de Matteis (1662–1728).

Images below left to right

A cat-shaped biscuit porcelain Kangxi nightlight holder

This *lapis lazuli* (a medium blue semi-precious stone) and enamel seal set bears the monogram of King Edward VII in diamonds. It was made by Collingwood & Co.

A box of pink stone in an egg shape by Fabergé

A devotional statue of Guandi (Kuan Tih), God of War, made in the Kangxi period (1662–1722). It has an opening in the back, where an offering to the god could be placed

Tea Room

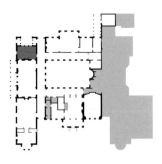

The Tea Room is in the style of Louis XVI, c.1785 and incorporates a series of late 18th-century pastoral landscapes. Probably Flemish, they are in the Rococo style of Fragonard or Boucher. The recreation of rooms in this style was popular with Mrs Greville's contemporaries. The Frick Collection in New York contains a similar room, the work of Charles Allom of White, Allom & Co. The feminine atmosphere and south-west aspect of Polesden's Tea Room was perfect for the ritual of afternoon tea.

Furniture

Most of the furniture listed in this room in 1943 was subsequently sold; it is now furnished with a mixture of items from Mrs Greville's Charles Street home and from the bedroom suites at Polesden Lacey. In the centre is a pair of small giltwood sofas covered in tapestry, c.1780. They are in the style of Georges Jacob, a leader of the Neo-classical style who received numerous royal commissions. Around the room are pieces of French furniture c.1760–1790 including dressing- and writing-tables.

'Maggie's teas were terrific, with great Georgian teapots and Indian or China tea, and muffins and cream cakes and silver kettles sending up their steam, and Queen Mary saying "Indian, if you please, and no sugar…"'

John Beverley Nichols,
Sweets and Twenties, 1958

Left and opposite
One of the eight pastoral landscapes in the Tea Room

Right This heart-shaped table de toilette is made of tulip wood. The top opens to reveal a mirror and two hinged side draws swing out to the sides (c.1715–1774)

'Tea is at 5 o'clock…and not at 5 minutes past…which means the Spanish Ambassador, who has gone for a walk down the yew avenue, hastily retraces his steps, and the Chancellor of the Exchequer hurries down the great staircase…and that the various ladies belonging to these gentlemen rise from their *chaise-longues*… and join the procession to the tea room.

'The tea pots, the cream jugs, the milk pots and the sugar basin are of Queen Anne silver; the tea service is Meissen and the doyleys, heavily monogrammed, are of Chantilly lace.'

John Beverley Nichols

Silver

The silver teapot on a stand to the right of the far window is by Marshall & Sons and is engraved with Mr McEwan's initials. It is one of the few pieces of modern silver that was not left to Mrs Greville's House Steward, Mr Bole, after her death. The rest of the silver in this room is significantly earlier. The salver is by Samuel Hood, London and is dated 1698; the shell-shaped cake basket is by Philip Garden, London, 1750; the silver teapots are early 18th-century English.

Top A view of the Tea Room

Above left A table set for tea

Billiard Room

The Billiard Room and adjacent Smoking Room and Gun Room form the masculine wing of the Edwardian house.

A gentleman's club in miniature, the room is dominated by the large Burrough and Watts billiard table. Around the fireplace are bookshelves, armchairs, a writing table and a games table.

This was the perfect atmosphere for Mrs Greville's male guests to relax in. They could talk politics, business and sport, and exchange fruity stories. The photographs illustrate some of Mrs Greville's favourite male guests: Prince Albert (later King George VI), Price George (2nd Duke of Cambridge) and Arthur Paget.

Above The Billiard Room was designed by Ambrose Poynter in 1903–5

Left A portrait of the Right Hon. William McEwan MP, Mrs Greville's father, by Walter William Ouless, 1901

Images below clockwise from top left

The Pleasures of Hope, William McTaggart, 1860

Sheep in Snow, Anton Mauve (date unknown)

Port of London, Samuel Bough, 1863

33

Tour of the House

Mr McEwan's pictures

As well as Dutch Old Master paintings William McEwan was a keen collector of 19th-century British and particularly Scottish artists. Many of these artists were themselves influenced by the 17th-century Dutch golden age that Mr McEwan admired.

Above the gramophone is Samuel Bough's *The Port of London*, 1863 (picture number 92). Although born in London, Bough was one of the driving forces in the development of 19th-century Scottish landscape painting. His particular interest was in the depiction of the fleeting effects of weather on landscape.

On the window wall are two works by Sir William McTaggart, *Seascape*, 1877 (117) and *The Pleasures of Hope*, 1860 (118). McTaggart's bold brushwork and colours show the influence of the Impressionists and echo Constable's and Turner's fascination with land and seascapes. Born on the Mull of Kintyre, he was admitted as an Associate of the Royal Scottish Academy at just 24. *Sheep in Snow* (95) by the far door is by Anton Mauve; related by marriage to Vincent van Gogh, he represents the 19th-century 'Hague School' of Dutch landscape painting.

At the far end of the room is a portrait of William McEwan, painted in 1901 by W. W. Ouless (93).

Smoking Room
Gun Room

Smoking Room

It was usual for an Edwardian country house to provide a smoking room where the gentlemen could retire after dinner. Smoking was considered risqué in front of the ladies and even after King Edward VII endorsed smoking in mixed society, Mrs Greville continued to call this the Smoking Room.

Photographs of Mrs Greville's house parties show that the male guests were rarely separated from their cigars and Turkish cigarettes. The inventory of Mrs Greville's own apartments confirms that she herself, at least in private, was a fairly heavy smoker, with numerous cigarette cases, holders and ashtrays among her personal possessions.

The décor

The wallpaper and curtains in this room date from the 1980s. The original wall colour is unknown but the overall colour scheme was red. The convex mirror above the fireplace is English, c.1830.

Right The fireplace in the Smoking Room

Gun Room

Originally for the storage and maintenance of guns for game shooting, the Gun Room showed no evidence of that function by 1943. The probate inventory shows it containing an invalid chair, a wicker armchair, an umbrella stand and two circular pouffes. The adjacent toilet, stacked with paintings, had also become wartime storage space.

Contents

The Gun Room contains a series of engravings illustrating the story of Don Quixote and an Aubusson tapestry c.1765–90. Also in the room is one of Mrs Greville's travelling trunks. By the door leading to the west lawn are two milk churns once used to deliver milk and cream from Polesden farm to Mrs Greville's London residence. They are inscribed, 'Hon Mrs Greville. Full to Victoria Station. Empty to Boxhill'.

Polesden in the First World War

From 1915 the entire West Wing of the house, including the Billiard Room, the Smoking Room and the Gun Room, was given over for use by convalescing officers. Mrs Greville's goddaughter Sonia Keppel wrote: 'Maggie Greville had turned most of her house…into a convalescent home to King Edward VII's Hospital for Officers. She had kept back the east side, and her own rooms on the south side for her private use.' As we might expect of Polesden Lacey, Sonia also notes that 'the Convalescents' Home… was run on luxurious lines'.

Sports

This room provided an entrance-hall for the gentlemen returning from sporting pursuits. The staircase beyond the glazed partition led straight to the bachelors' bedrooms and there was a convenient washroom next door. Maggie Greville seems to have favoured the more modern sports of tennis and golf as opposed to shooting.

Above The Gun Room, looking north-west

The Gardens

The gardens' setting at Polesden Lacey is spectacular, perched on a chalk ridge and taking in views southwards towards the wooded slopes of Ranmore Common and the valley below.

In the past, there would also have been views to Box Hill to the east which over time we hope to restore.

History of the garden – Edwardian floral exuberance

There are approximately 12 hectares (30 acres) of garden to explore at Polesden. What we see today very much echoes the glorious heyday of the Edwardian period and Mrs Greville's time here, encapsulating the flamboyance and exuberance of her era. One can imagine the sound of music coming from the house on summer evenings mingled with laughter, merriment and the chink of champagne glasses.

This garden was a playground for the rich and famous in the early part of the 20th century. Just a stone's throw from London, it was pure escapism from city life.

Mrs Greville's garden

Many of the planting schemes, particularly to the west of the house, are the result of Mrs Greville's own personal vision for her garden. She extended the walled garden and created the Herbaceous Borders, the Rose Garden and the Rockery. She even created a Pet Cemetery for her beloved dogs (see page 57). Most of the changes she made to the garden were completed before 1914.

'A Peep of Beautiful Distance'
Diarist Joseph Farington, 1803

A garden of two halves – the formal and informal

Although there has been a house and garden on this site since the Middle Ages, Polesden's recorded horticultural history covers the last 400 years. It is this rich horticultural past which gives the garden its unique charm. There is a blend of informal walkways, pleasure gardens and wooded copses to the east of the property; to the west are the more formal, colourful and elaborate gardens including the walled gardens and the productive areas.

Looking after the garden

The exposed hilltop site and thin chalky soil has always made it difficult to garden here. However, previous owners and their teams of gardeners have overcome adversity by importing rich, fertile soil in which plants can grow, and by creating shelter belts and walled gardens to protect the garden, making this a truly glorious setting.

Left Looking out onto Ranmore Common

Opposite Polesden's cherubim sundial, with a view beyond

Below A view through the rose pergolas of the walled garden, and on to the lawn

Walnut Lawn and Weeping Elm Lawn

Some of the most notable trees in the garden are the sweet chestnuts (*Castania sativa*) flanking the Walnut Lawn and Weeping Elm Lawn. Probably about 150 years old, their magnificent gnarled and twisted trunks line the northern approach to the house.

The Walnut Lawn was originally the site of a walled garden but is now planted with ornamental trees, including an attractive foxglove tree (*Paulownia tomentosa*) which produces large purple flowers in summer.

The Walnut Lawn is lined on the other side by lime trees; during summer their flowers provide a fragrant, sweet scent to visitors entering the garden from under the Water Tower.

The elm trees on Weeping Elm Lawn sadly succumbed to Dutch Elm disease and now have been replaced by other ornamental trees, including an American sweet gum (*Liquidambar styraciflua*), with attractive autumn colours and scented foliage. Along the eastern edge of the lawn 20,000 daffodil bulbs have been planted, creating a stunning display in spring.

Above A beech-lined track in autumn adjacent to the drive

Orchards, copses and woodland walks

Aerial photos from the 1930s and 40s show rows of tightly packed trees, indicating that this was once a productive fruit orchard. The National Trust has since planted crab apple trees to emulate this Edwardian feature in the garden. Late spring is the best time to admire the crab blossom, while in autumn the trees' colourful fruits provide an extra interest in the garden.

Preserve Copse is an attractive woodland area towards the east of the property. It is one of the few areas that has acidic soil, meaning it can be planted with exciting woodland trees and shrubs that thrive in those conditions – rhododendrons, camellias and magnolias. Recent planting has focused on autumn colour with an exciting range of Japanese maples (*Acer palmatum*), stewartias and varieties of silver birch. In spring time, the rhododendrons come into their own with a stunning range of colours, while the floor is carpeted with a mass of bluebells. If visiting at the right time of year, there are clumps of lesser spotted orchids to be found among the woodlands too.

Large specimens of trees can be found in this area including Douglas fir (*Pseudotsuga menziesii*), giant redwood (*Sequoiadendron giganteum*) and the California redwood (*Sequoia sempervirens*).

Right This sweet gum *Liquidambar styraciflua* is one of the key feature trees on Weeping Elm Lawn. It looks at its best in autumn when its leaves give a display of fiery crimsons, oranges and golds

Admiral's Walk and Squirrel's Corner
Long Walk, Nun's Walk, Pinetum

Admiral's Walk and Squirrel's Corner

Possibly named after Admiral Geary, an 18th-century owner of Polesden Lacey, this woodland walk runs east/west along the bottom of Preserve Copse and just above Theatre Lawn.

Half-way along the track is a bird hide where visitors can try to spot any rare or interesting species, including great spotted woodpeckers, nuthatches, long-tail tits and bullfinches (depending on the season). Following the avenue eastwards, away from the house, eventually leads out onto the estate; by following a path south, visitors will come to the play area called Squirrel's Corner. This is an attractive wooded glade with a range of rustic play equipment for children (and adults) to enjoy. There is also an impressive sculptural bench, created using a chainsaw. It features griffins to link in with the limestone statues on the South Lawn and outside the Rose Garden.

Long Walk, Nun's Walk, Pinetum

The Long Walk (sometimes referred to as Sheridan's Walk) was possibly created by Sir Francis Geary around 1761. Below the yew hedge is a flint ha-ha. At the east end are six Doric columns which create a focal point. They were originally on the front of the house and were moved to their present position in 1903 during the ownership of Sir Clinton Dawkins. The walk is about 500m long and the topiary of the yew hedge, which continues along the bottom of the South Lawn, was 'castellated' until the 1960s.

Right A portrait of Admiral Sir Francis Geary

Far right The atmospheric Nun's Walk 'tunnel'

Opposite The Long Walk in 1915

Nun's Walk

Nun's Walk is an incredible tunnel created out of yew trees running parallel with the Long Walk. Originally the yew would have been hedging on either side of the walkway, but over the last few decades the trees have grown inwards to create this unique tunnel effect. It is particularly popular with children and of course is great for creating that 'spooky' effect around Hallowe'en time. It is also a popular alternative to the Long Walk in the winter months, as it offers some shelter from the rain.

Pinetum

The towering conifers in the Pinetum to the south-east of the house are a great example of trees that flourish in impoverished chalky soil. If you look carefully here you will come across the grave of a dog named 'Mr Snooks'. He belonged to a Belgian ambassador and sadly died while his master was staying at Polesden Lacey as one of Mrs Greville's guests. Mrs Greville allowed the ambassador to choose a spot to bury his beloved pet.

Golf Course
Lawns
Front of the House

Edwardian golf

Golf was a very popular pastime in the
Edwardian period, and of course, Mrs Greville
had to have her very own golf course. Many of
her guests would have taken the opportunity
to enjoy a round on the estate, including
Sir Winston Churchill.

The majority of the course was in Golf
Course Field (the huge field on the left when
approaching the property from Bookham), but
a section of it also wrapped around the back of
Preserve Copse and on to Theatre Lawn
towards the front of the house. The remains of
a couple of golf bunkers can still be seen on the
north side of Bagden Drive. The celebrated
golfer and course-designer Harry Vardon
(1870–1937) is alleged to have created the golf
course for Mrs Greville, but there is no
significant evidence to support this, though
there is evidence that he played on the course.

Left Visitors on Polesden
Lacey's golf course, 1916

Theatre Lawn

Theatre Lawn is so called because of the
outdoor theatre that was constructed there in
1951 by the Bookham Commons Association.
It is still regularly used for outdoor
performances in summer.

Roman Bath Lawn

To the west of the South Lawn is the Roman
Bath Lawn – a sloping grass area enclosed by
formal yew hedging. At the foot of the slope is
an antique bath, and on each side is a cherub
statue. The National Trust has been restoring
the view by cutting back the encroaching laurel
hedging at the bottom of the garden. The
archway to the west leads to the Upper Sunken
Garden and was created in 1923 for the future
George VI and his wife Elizabeth.

Front of the House

At the end of Bagden Drive, at the front of the
house, is a gravelled forecourt surrounded by
large golden yew tightly clipped into spheres.
There is a 15th-century Venetian wellhead in
the centre of the forecourt, though at least
until 1910 this was a sundial. The wellhead was
moved here at a later date.

The surrounding walls of the house are
clothed with climbers including winter
jasmine (*Jasminum nudiflorum*) and Chinese
wisteria (*Wisteria sinensis*).

Bagden Drive

Bagden Drive cuts through Theatre Lawn and leads to the front of the house. It was created by Sir Walter Farquhar, Polesden Lacey's Victorian owner, as the main access to the property. It was a particularly useful link to Westhumble train station at the foot of Box Hill and became Mrs Greville's favourite route to and from her property.

South Lawn

The South Lawn is without doubt the most popular area of the garden with visitors today. Quintessentially English with its breathtaking views and verdant lawns, it's the perfect place to relax in a deckchair and enjoy a picnic.

Ronald and Maggie Greville's elaborate plans for this area were an Italianate landscape including formal terracing, statues and water features; they were never fulfilled, although the designs can be seen in the Blue Cloakroom in the house. There also used to be a large stone fountain and pool in front of the house; on a dry day the outline of it can be seen in the lawn.

Left The South Lawn is the perfect place to relax

Above Bagden Drive in autumn

Sunken Gardens
Rockery
Croquet

Upper Sunken Garden and Lower Sunken Garden

Walking through the archway from the Roman Bath Lawn takes visitors into a less frequented area of the garden, the Upper Sunken Garden. In winter there is a spectacular display of the white-stemmed ornamental bramble (*Rubus cockburnianus*). The stems are left until March before being cut down to the ground by the garden team, to regrow again during the summer. The bank that borders the northern side of the garden has smoke bushes (*Cotinus coggygria*) which turn fiery red and orange in autumn.

Opposite the Rockery stand two striking ornamental trees. One of them is the handkerchief or dove tree (*Davidia involucrata*) which produces stunning white bracts in summer. The other is *Liriodendron tulipifera*, the tulip tree, which has unusual shaped leaves and yellow tulip-shaped flowers.

Below this garden is the Lower Sunken Garden. In Mrs Greville's day this was an attractive woodland walk with terraced footpaths. It has been closed to the public for a number of years but is now being restored to its former glory. The Jubilee Bridge at the bottom of the Rockery leads around to the New Kitchen Garden.

Above left A tulip tree *Liriodendron tulipifera* in autumn

Above right The Sunken Garden with maple *Acer* trees in autumn colours

Left The statue of Diana can be seen at the western end of the Croquet Lawn

landscape gardeners, James Pulham and Son. However, rumour has it that Mrs Greville had a falling out with the contractors and the work was never completed. Research has shown that it was probably not Pulhams, but J. Cheal and Son who finally carried out some of the work. At the top of the Rockery is a lead statue of Diana the Huntress, Goddess of the Hunt (as well as of the moon and birthing), clutching her bow and arrow with a dead stag at her feet.

Tree ferns (*Dicksonia antarctica*) have been planted along the western edge of the Rockery. These thrive under the leafy canopy of the lime avenue that leads up the hill towards the Winter Garden.

Croquet

Just below the Herbaceous Borders there are four croquet lawns. In Mrs Greville's time this area was used as a lawn tennis court. In the south-west corner of the croquet area is a bladdernut (*Staphylea pinnata*) that has attractive white flowers in spring, and later produces quirky-looking fruit.

Below The Rockery

Rockery

The Rockery has been restored to its Edwardian heyday, using funds raised by a property raffle. Tiny sweet-smelling narcissus and other bulbs such as gentian and crocus carpet the floor below the Rockery and can be found growing in the nooks and crevices, while larger shrubs create areas of interest in the rock face. The rock is made from Westmorland limestone and the white stone 'mulch' is Cotswold chippings.

Mrs Greville had plans to transform the entire length of the bank below the Croquet Lawn into a rockery with an informal lake in the middle of the grass in the Upper Sunken Garden; designs were drawn up by the famous

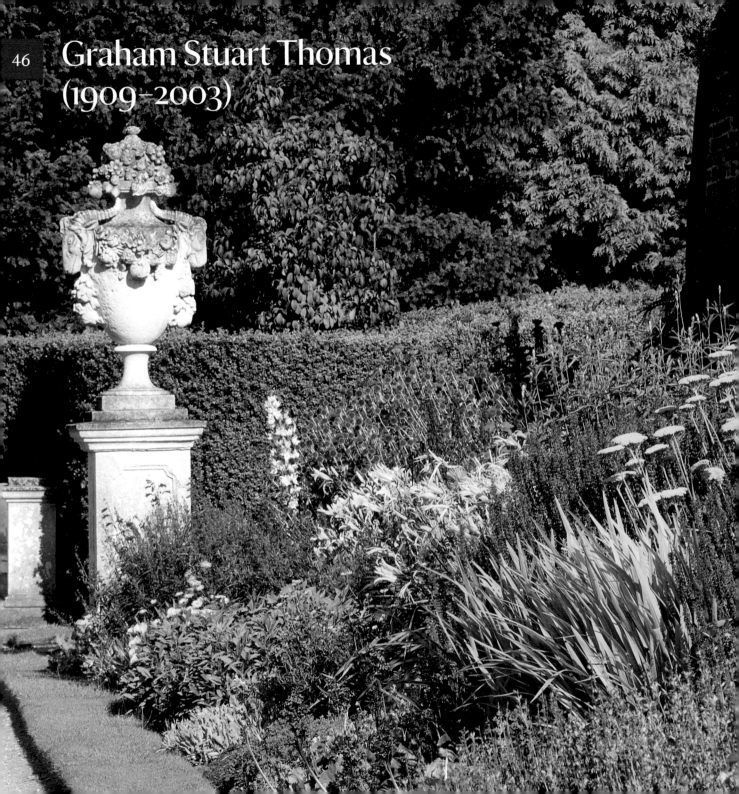

Graham Stuart Thomas
(1909–2003)

Although he is relatively unknown outside horticultural circles, Graham Stuart Thomas was one of the most influential gardeners of the late 20th century. Known as GST to friends and colleagues, his name is synonymous with roses, but he was also a prolific garden writer, nurseryman, plantsman, botanical artist and garden designer. For 30 years he was Chief Garden Adviser for the National Trust, and as such, was responsible for many of the greatest garden designs in the country.

The rose garden GST designed at Mottisfont Abbey in Hampshire is considered to be the greatest in the world, and has become a Mecca for rose lovers during the summer months. Polesden Lacey is very lucky to have a number of GST's designs, including the Herbaceous Borders, the Rose Garden and the Winter Garden. Other horticultural gems he designed include the 'hot and cool' herbaceous borders in front of Cliveden in Berkshire and the Edwardian-style borders at Lyme Park in Cheshire (both National Trust).

GST received numerous gardening accolades throughout his career, including the Royal Horticultural Society's Veitch Memorial Medal and its Victoria Medal of Honour. He also achieved a lifetime achievement award from the Garden Writers' Guild in 1996. In 1975 he was awarded the OBE for his dedication to horticulture and his work for the National Trust.

A few plants are named after him, the most popular being the climbing rose 'Graham Thomas' and the honeysuckle *Lonicera periclymenum* 'Graham Thomas'.

Books written by Graham Stuart Thomas include:
The Old Shrub Roses (1955)
Colour in the Winter Garden (1957)
Shrub Roses of Today (1962)
Climbing Roses Old and New (1965)
Perennial Garden Plants (1975)
Plants for Ground Cover (1977)
The Art of Planting (1984)
Complete Flower Paintings and Drawings of Graham Stuart Thomas (1987)
Cuttings from My Garden Notebooks (1997)
Treasured Perennials (1999)
Three Gardens of Pleasant Flowers: With Notes on Their Design, Maintenance and Plants (2001)
The Garden Through the Year (2002)

Below The eponymous
Graham Thomas
climbing rose

Left A view of the western end of Graham Stuart Thomas's Herbaceous Border

Above Graham Stuart Thomas

Herbaceous Borders
Winter Garden

Herbaceous Borders

The mixed borders are some of the longest in the country, stretching 150 metres on each side. Their style is typical of the Edwardian fashion using flamboyant herbaceous perennials combined with exuberant colours and textures. There is a mix of traditional plants and shrubs with ornamental grasses and exotic-looking plants. At the back of the borders the walls are clothed in colourful wall-shrubs and climbers.

The South Border

During the war years the South Border was turned over to vegetable production as part of the Dig For Victory campaign. The National Trust grassed this a few years later to reduce labour costs. It remained this way until 2011 when it was opened up as part of a restoration programme. For the first couple of years our National Trust gardeners grew an impressive springtime display of tulips as part of a tulip festival. It has now been restored to a double-sided Edwardian border.

The North Border

Graham Stuart Thomas (GST) redesigned this border in 1973. One of his signature plant combinations is the stunning deep yellow of the yarrow 'Gold Plate' (*Achillea filipendulina*) contrasted with the deep purple of the *Salvia x superba* (a type of sage). This combination has been repeated throughout the planting to create recurring crescendos of interest.

GST also liked to use plants with interesting foliage throughout the borders. In this design he used sea kale (*Crambe maritima*) and yuccas to regularly punctuate the planting scheme.

The Spring Borders

Walking around the corner at the west end of the Herbaceous Borders are the Spring Borders, which were designed to come into flower earlier in the year. At the end is Gardener's Cottage. This unusual little house

Left The Herbaceous Borders, looking towards the house

with its zig-zag chimney and attractive gabling
was originally the Head Gardener's cottage. It
is now available for holiday lets.

Winter Garden

This small garden is one of the most
significant areas of the whole estate, yet is not
associated with Mrs Greville or the Edwardian
period. It was designed by Graham Stuart
Thomas (GST) in the 1970s (see pages 46–7)
and is believed to be the only example of a
winter garden designed by him.

Between late January and early February the
central section of the garden is carpeted with
yellow aconites (*Eranthis*) under the three trees
which are Persian ironwoods (*Parrotia persica*).
These trees are so named because their wood is
extremely dense and sinks in water.

In the surrounding beds are unusual winter
flowering shrubs such as the buffalo berry
(*Shepherdia argentea*). From late autumn onwards
the ground erupts with colourful bulbs including
narcissus, scilla and crocus. There is also a large
snowdrop display showing over twenty varieties.
One of the most striking aspects of the garden is the
beautiful fragrance in winter from plants such as
Christmas box (*Sarcococca hookeriana* var. *digyna*)
towards the south of the garden with wintersweet
(*Chimonanthus praecox*) and Nepalese paper plant
(*Daphne bholua*) towards its northern end.

Above Aconites (*Eranthis*)
in the Winter Garden
provide year-round colour

Lavender and Iris Gardens
New Kitchen Garden

Lavender and Iris Gardens

The planting in these two gardens is simple but effective, each one focusing on just one type of plant. Both gardens are enclosed on one side by flint walls built as extensions to the 19th-century walled gardens. The walls have planting pockets where sedums and trailing aubretia thrive. The gardens are surrounded on the other three sides by clipped formal yew hedges.

The Lavender Garden has a border running parallel with it, on the other side of the east yew hedge, called the Peony Border – another introduction by Graham Stuart Thomas in the 1970s; it is edged with ruby-coloured sedums.

Traditionally there would have been bedding plants in the middle of the Lavender Garden, but now golden thyme takes the stage, creating a stunning contrast with the blue lavender. The thyme variety is called *Thymus pulegioides* 'Bertram Anderson' which has the habit of knitting together to create a 'thyme lawn'.

The varieties of English lavender, one for each corner, are all associated with the Edwardian period: *Lavandula angustifolia* 'Hidcote', 'Munstead', 'Granny's Bouquet' and 'Ashdown Forest'. Both the Iris and Lavender Gardens feature moon windows (*claires-voies*) which frame views to the world beyond; when seen from outside, they frame the central sculpture in each garden. The Lavender Garden centrepiece is a statue called 'Dancing Faun'.

The Iris Garden comes into its own in early summer when its collection of bearded irises flower. Varieties include iris (*Iris pallida* var. *dalmatica*) 'Prosper Laugier', 'Cleo', 'Moonlight' and 'Constance Mayer'. The central sculpture is an armillary sphere.

Left Bearded iris in May

Right The Lavender Garden

Opposite The New Kitchen Garden in 1915 or 16

New Kitchen Garden

The sunken lane that the thatched bridge crosses was constructed in 1861 and divides the formal gardens from the surrounding rural landscape. If you look carefully in the flint wall just past the bridge, the date 1861 can be seen. Mrs Greville decided to move her kitchen garden from the walled garden to this area on the other side of the sunken lane.

The New Kitchen Garden was divided into four quarters and had wide flower borders planted along the east-west axis. There was an orchard, an area for cold frames (a tool used like a mini greenhouse) and beds for growing vegetables. Some of the original damson trees can still be seen along the eastern edge of the garden. It continued to be used as a kitchen garden by the National Trust but was abandoned in the 1960s owing to labour costs. It was a Christmas tree plantation for a while, and then in the 1980s was planted with rows of lime trees, the borders edged with cherry trees. The National Trust gardeners are gradually removing some of the lime trees to restore the New Kitchen Garden and to encourage sunlight into the area, which in turn will create a richer biodiversity.

Cold Frame Yard and Potting Shed Orchard

Cold Frame Yard and Potting Shed

During the Edwardian period, cold frames would have been used to force food in spring into early cropping, or to extend the season in autumn. Mrs Greville liked to have her strawberries forced early under glass to impress her house guests. Cold frames were also used to force sweet-smelling violets so that they could be brought indoors to make the house fragrant during the winter. Polesden Lacey's produce and flowers were also sent up to Mrs Greville's London house in Mayfair.

The outbuildings housed the boiler for the glasshouses which used 30 to 40 tonnes of coke per annum. There were a range of glasshouses here during Mrs Greville's time, but sadly they were destroyed by a Second World War bomb. Another outbuilding was used as a mushroom house.

The Potting Shed is evocative of the Edwardian period and gives a real sense of what it was like to be a gardener during this era. The back section was used by Henry Smith, Head Gardener between 1938 and 1962, as his office. His roll-top desk and safe can still be seen today.

Behind the restored cold frames is an area for growing cut flowers which is still used today to supply floral displays in the house. On the other side of the path is the Vegetable Plot which produces seasonal crops, used by the chefs in the Granary Café.

Orchard and its chickens

Walking past the cold frames and productive gardens leads to an attractive orchard where chickens are kept. Mrs Greville kept poultry on the estate and so they have been reinstated in the garden.

Of particular interest is the Dorking breed, which has five toes instead of the usual four. The Dorking cockerel is the emblem of the local town of Dorking and its image can be seen throughout the locality. It is an historic breed, possibly introduced by the Romans, and is famous for its dual qualities, being good for both meat and eggs. Dorkings were particularly popular in Victorian and Edwardian times, and Queen Victoria was said to insist on having only white eggs from Dorking hens. The chickens come in a variety of colours, the most sought-after being the silver-grey, but there are also dark, red and white Dorkings.

Above The Head Gardener's desk in the Polesden Lacey Potting Shed

Left Cold frames propped open in the garden

THE CELEBRATED
DORKING SAUCE,

For Game, Chops, Hashes, Hot and Cold Meat, Fish, Soups, Gravies, Curries, &c.

This delicious Condiment, which possesses a peculiar and agreeable piquancy, is, from the superiority of its zest, more generally useful than any other yet introduced, and is besides, from its valuable stomachic qualities, greatly calculated to facilitate digestion.

Prepared only by
E. & F. DURANT, LATE **HARRISON,**
Chemists, Dorking,

And may be obtained of all respectable Chemists and Grocers throughout the Kingdom.

PRICE ONE SHILLING.

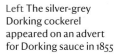

Left The silver-grey Dorking cockerel appeared on an advert for Dorking sauce in 1855

Below Alex Valsecchi demonstrates winter pruning at Yew Tree Farm

Right at the end of the garden is an apple orchard, planted with local varieties mainly from Surrey and Sussex, such as Claygate Pearmain, Byfleet Seedling and Crawley Beauty. This was known as Home Farm Orchard in the Edwardian period, and one of the surviving trees from that era can be seen in the far west corner of the orchard. It is a Rosemary Russet, considered by apple connoisseurs to be one of the most flavoursome of all the 'russet' types.

Rose Garden

'Won't you come into the garden?
I would like my roses to see you.'

Playwright Richard Brinsley Sheridan,
who bought Polesden Lacey in 1797

This is the highlight of the garden at Polesden
Lacey. In the height of summer the floral
display and fragrance encapsulated in this
walled garden are breathtaking. The Rose
Garden is divided into quarters and was built
by a popular Edwardian landscape company
called J. Cheal and Son. It has about fifty
different varieties of rose and includes a mix
of traditional Edwardian roses, modern hybrid
teas and floribundas.

What was here before?

Before Mrs Greville's time, this garden would
have been a traditional fruit and vegetable
garden. Opinion is divided as to why Mrs
Greville decided to move her kitchen garden to
the other side of the thatched bridge. Some
claim that the fruit and veg weren't glamorous
enough to impress her important and royal
guests. Others believe that she needed more
space to grow sufficient food for her staff and
frequent house parties. Either way, Mrs Greville
took great interest in the crops growing in her
gardens. The produce grown at Polesden Lacey
frequently won local gardening competitions
as well as supplying her guests and numerous
staff both here and at her London house.

The pergola

Made from sweet chestnut and with a natural,
rustic feel, the pergola is typical of the Arts and
Crafts style so prevalent in the Edwardian era.
In the summer it's adorned with climbers and
rambling roses, many of which were popular
Edwardian varieties such as 'Dorothy Perkins'
and 'American Pillar'. The original pergola
supported a large wooden dome over the
centre of the garden which added height and
gave an imposing sense of opulence and
grandeur. The outer beds are filled with a range
of shrub roses, including some rare varieties
that Graham Stuart Thomas introduced in the
1970s and 1980s.

Left Evening light shines
on a cherub statue in the
east corner of the Rose
Garden

Right A view of the
Rose Garden

Opposite The Rose
Garden, including the
water tower

The Water Tower

The Water Tower was built between 1903 and 1905 and was used to irrigate the garden. The water was pumped up from a deep bore hole below the garden. The Chinese wisteria on the wall is thought to be over a hundred years old and its attractive blue racemes perfume the air during late spring.

The Well

Creating a focal point in the centre of the garden is a 14th-century Venetian well from the Palazzo Morosini Sagredo. The Sagredo family motto, 'When God Pleases', appears on the wellhead. It refers to a period when they fell on hard times and hoped their family would flourish once more.

What isn't here?

There was also a greenhouse on the south side of the walled garden that was used to grow tropical plants and housed a grapevine; sadly this fell into disrepair and was removed in the 1970s.

The Ladies' Garden
The Pets' Cemetery

The Ladies' Garden

This was Mrs Greville's favourite place to sit and enjoy the view although much of that view has now been obscured. National Trust gardeners are gradually trying to restore those glimpses of Ranmore Common and the woods beyond by removing some of the overgrown trees and shrubs.

It's fitting that Mrs Greville's grave is here, just a short distance from where her beloved dogs are buried. It is a sheltered, secluded area of the garden, surrounded by tightly clipped yew hedging and with the walled garden to the west. At the back of the Ladies' Garden are terracotta statuettes of the four seasons.

Just south of the Ladies' Garden is a black mulberry tree (*Morus nigra*) planted by Prince Charles in 1988. It replaced the original tree, planted by Edward VII in 1907, which had been damaged in the great storm of 1987. Looking back towards the west side of the house, the wall is clothed with a yellow-scented climbing rose called *Rosa banksiae* 'Lutea'.

MARGARET HELEN GREVILLE D B E

Above The Pets' Cemetery, with the grave of Edward VII's Airedale, 'Caeser' in the centre

Left Mrs Greville's grave can be seen in the Ladies' Garden

Top Two of Mrs
Greville's beloved
dogs play in the garden

Right Mrs Greville with
Tyne, one of her dogs

The Pets' Cemetery

One of the quirkier aspects of Polesden Lacey is the Pets' Cemetery. It's located towards the east of the Ladies' Garden where Mrs Greville herself rests. She loved her dogs and is often seen in photos with them. In total, there are 17 dogs buried in the cemetery; each one is marked with a gravestone with the dog's name carved upon it.

All the house staff being expected to turn out for a dog's funeral shows how much importance Mrs Greville attached to her beloved pets.

'Apparently, Mrs Greville knew of Molly's talent for needlework and asked her specially to make a cushion suitable for one of her dogs, who had just passed away, to be laid to rest on. The cushion was made and the butler placed the dead dog on to it. All the staff were then told to follow behind the butler, in procession, to the dog cemetery.'

Molly the housemaid's nephew remembers how her talent was put to use to honour one of Mrs Greville's dogs

The Estate

The Polesden Lacey estate sits in the centre of stunning countryside. In almost every direction there are breathtaking views including the London skyline to the north and the rolling hills of the north downs to the south. It is as rich in historical features as it is in wildlife and biodiversity.

Stretching to about 560 hectares (1400 acres), the estate is predominantly a mix of chalk grassland and deciduous woodland, although there are patches of coniferous plantations. There are over 26 miles of footpaths and bridleways for visitors to discover and those wishing to explore further can easily get to Box Hill, Leith Hill and other beauty spots on foot or by bike.

Managing woodland
The woodlands are managed by a small team of National Trust rangers and volunteers. Much of the team's time is spent keeping the grassy woodland 'rides' clear of trees, to maintain the diverse habitats that make this area special.

New additions
The estate includes Ranmore Common, 200 hectares (500 acres) to the south of the property, which was gifted to the National Trust in 1959. Despite Surrey being the most wooded county in England, Ranmore Common is considered to be the last remaining complete 200-hectare woodland in the country. The most spectacular time of year is in the spring when bluebells, a key indicator of ancient woodland, carpet the forest floor.

The importance of animals
242 hectares (600 acres) of the Polesden estate are managed by two tenant farmer families. The Grays have been managing Goldstone Farm since Mrs Greville's time and have built up an award-winning herd of Ayrshire cows. Beef cattle and sheep graze Polesden Farm, providing meat for our café. Much of the farmland is managed under stewardship schemes which promote good environmental management.

Above The estate in autumn

Left Polesden's bluebells tell us these woods have been here for over 400 years

In addition, the grazing of livestock plays an important role in the conservation of the chalk grassland; the shorter grass encourages a greater diversity of wildlife into the meadows. There is an incredible richness of wildlife to look out for including badgers, deer, butterflies; 12 of the 16 species of bats in the United Kingdom have been recorded on the estate.

Historic buildings and places

Numerous historic buildings can be found on the estate. Bagden Farm, to the east of the estate, is thought to be on the site of a Roman villa, complete with vineyard.

The oldest building, Tanner's Hatch, nestles in the valley between Polesden Lacey and Ranmore Woods. It is a timber-framed cottage dating back to 1614. The word 'hatch' implies it was originally a gateway where drovers would enter onto the common to graze their livestock. It is now managed by the Youth Hostel Association.

Other features of interest include the Italianate bridge built by Sir Clinton Dawkins in 1902 and the chalkpit near Freehold Wood which was worked in the 1800s to make lime for building materials or fertiliser for the fields.

Left Tenant farmer Steve Conisbee with his herd of beef cattle

Above Tanners Hatch, now looked after by the Youth Hostel Association

Servants

Maintaining Polesden's luxurious lifestyle required an army of servants.

Top Frederick Hart, Mrs Greville's chauffeur, and his family

Bottom Mrs Greville's personal secretary, a chauffeur and maids, photographed in the Inner Courtyard

Guests at Polesden Lacey could lounge on wicker chairs under the shaded loggias, try a sport, meet the right people or sample an endless parade of food. They had the illusion of complete freedom combined with the comfort of a highly orchestrated social gathering.

Mrs Greville employed skilled staff who ensured the smooth running of Polesden Lacey and her London home in Charles Street. The hall boy, the groom and the gardener, the highly qualified cook or chef, the personal secretary, the golf pro and the ever-present Mr Bole, House Steward at Polesden Lacey, all played their part.

Top Frederick Hart, Mrs Greville's chauffeur, and his family

Bottom Mrs Greville's personal secretary, a chauffeur and maids, photographed in the Inner Courtyard

Changing times

Mrs Greville owned Polesden Lacey from the Edwardian period to the Second World War, a time of dramatic change in the employment market. The story of the Hart family at Polesden reflects the changing roles and expectations of Mrs Greville's servants.

Frederick Hart was employed by Mrs Greville's father as a groom, but with the rise in popularity of the motorcar, he came to Polesden Lacey to be Mrs Greville's chauffeur. Two of his daughters, when they reached their early teens, were sent to Charles Street to serve as maids. Marie settled in well but modern-thinking Lorna did not. When asked to polish the coal scuttles both inside and out she challenged the housekeeper – wasn't it a waste of her time as the footmen would only put coal into it again? Further disagreements and questions led to Lorna's dismissal; she went on to get a job with Sainsbury's. The Edwardian servant life led by her father did not have the same appeal for a young lady in the 1920s.

The drunken butler

Accounts of the footmen and butlers given by a number of Mrs Greville's guests seem like caricatures from a P.G. Woodhouse novel. If true, they suggest Mrs Greville was more lenient towards her upper servants than her housekeeper was with a new maid.

'[Mrs Greville] noticed that the butler was swaying ominously at the other end of the room [and] she wrote on a scrap of paper, "You are drunk. Leave the room at once" and gave the note to the footman to pass to the offender. When the butler read the message he put the piece of paper on the salver, staggered across the room and presented it to Sir Austen Chamberlain.'

Historian Sir Charles Petrie, 3rd Baronet

Above **Harry Alibone,** a dairy worker, outside his workspace

Above right **The chef and staff in the kitchen,** c.1909

Stable Courtyard

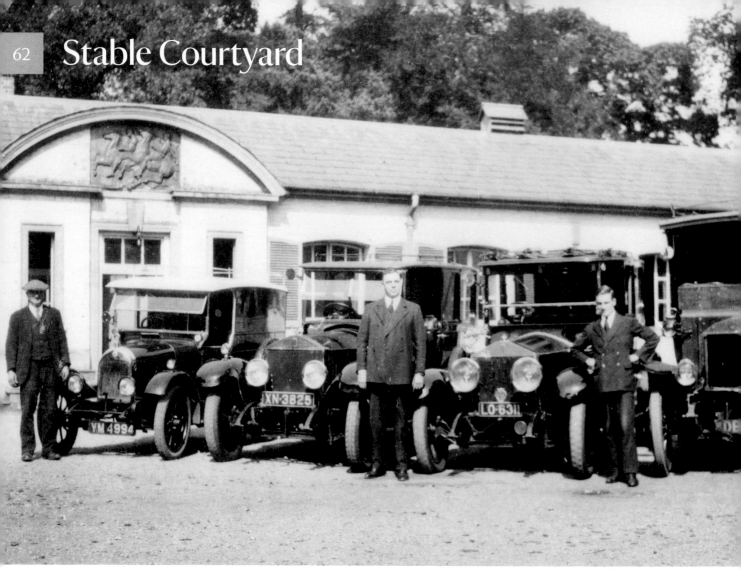

The facilities provided for Polesden Lacey's servants were the height of modernity and the Stable Courtyard is a model Edwardian service space, bordered by cottages for staff and tenants.

In 1907 *The Engineer* magazine ran an article entitled 'Engineering of a Country House' in which Polesden Lacey was used as an exemplar of how engineering could be used to deliver 'the requirements of comfort and hygiene demanded today in country houses'.

Designing the area

Ambrose Poynter designed most of the courtyard we see today for Clinton Dawkins between 1903 and 1905. It contains a central water tower providing water pressure to the mansion. To the right of the water tower is the 'motor house', which originally had two inspection pits; it is now our Visitor Reception. On the other side of the water tower, the 1905 plan shows the coach house. The north side of the courtyard, where the

Above Chauffeurs and mechanics with Mrs Greville's fleet of cars

shop is now located, was originally taken up entirely by stabling. As the number of horses kept at Polesden Lacey reduced, Mrs Greville converted the eastern end into a servants' social club. Facilities included a library and a billiard table (now in the Billiard Room in the main house).

The western side of the courtyard, once a barn, was reordered by Sir Ambrose Macdonald Poynter to contain the hay and corn stores and mixing room needed for state-of-the-art stables. In between the stables and the fodder stores was accommodation for some of the outdoor staff. Groom Arthur Thompson remembers: 'I had a bedroom, and a little bathroom; next to me was the golf professional, Len Bates, young…nice fellow. If it was a nice summer evening, especially when Her Ladyship was away, we'd go and have a round of golf.'

Above right **This photograph from September 1905 shows the work done to the harness room and stables by Ambrose Poynter**

Right A chauffeur with car

'The fish is good, the meat is fine,
 No need to praise the luscious wine!
The beds and linen 'beat the band',
The water's hot, the butler's grand.

There's golf and tennis and every game,
What other comfort can I name?
 But why speak of wine & meat?
'Tis our hostess whose [sic] so sweet.'

Lord Plunket

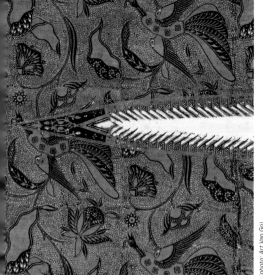

(photo: Art Van Go)

(photo: M. Wicks)

(photo: Art Van Go)

CU00662749

BATIK TRANSITIONS

FROM CLASSIC TO CONTEMPORARY

COMPILED AND EDITED BY DIANE GAFFNEY
INTRODUCTION BY NOEL DYRENFORTH

THE BATIK GUILD, IN CELEBRATION OF ITS TWENTIETH ANNIVERSARY, IS PRESENTING A COMPREHENSIVE EXHIBITION "BATIK TRANSITIONS – FROM CLASSIC TO CONTEMPORARY" IN SIX VENUES THROUGHOUT ENGLAND FROM SEPTEMBER 2006 TO MAY 2007. BESIDES BEING A SHOWCASE FOR THE BEST CONTEMPORARY WORK, SELECTED PIECES FROM PRIVATE COLLECTIONS OF TRADITIONAL BATIKS ADD A HISTORIC PERSPECTIVE. IN ADDITION, A SERIES OF HANDS-ON WORKSHOPS HAVE BEEN ARRANGED WITH THE RESPECTIVE GALLERIES AND MUSEUM EDUCATIONAL PROGRAMMES.

THIS SERIES OF EXHIBITIONS IS LIKELY TO BE SEEN BY THOUSANDS. MANY, I HOPE, WILL NOT ONLY ENJOY THE WORK BUT WILL BE INSPIRED TO TRY THEIR HAND AT BATIK.

The Batik Guild was launched in the summer of 1986 when I chaired a small committee of students and organised a newsletter and constitution. A plan for exhibitions and workshops was devised to promote batik as an accessible creative art process. Response was immediate and impressive. A total of 120 members signed up for the first newsletter, published in October 1986. Art and adult education colleges soon made batik part of their curriculum; teachers from primary school level and upwards were captivated by the craft.

The first Guild exhibition was in April 1989 at the Camden Art Centre, London, and showed a wide mix of individuality and skill. The public's preconceptions were challenged and reviewers applauded. In retrospect this exhibition, above any others, acted as a benchmark. It offered a fresh appraisal of an ancient craft. A number of exhibitions followed in quick succession including The Swiss Cottage Library Gallery in 1991 and The National Theatre Gallery in 1994. As a consequence of the increasing awareness of art textiles the membership rose to over 250.

By the mid '90s, international links were fostered and individual members exhibited and attended batik conferences in China, Japan, Indonesia and, more recently, Boston, USA. It was here that one of our members, Heather Gatt, won a top prize in the international exhibition.

A full programme continued throughout the '90s in the UK, promoting the public's concerns for the preservation of hand skills and creativity. However, as a result of the narrowing of state education services batik – in common with the arts generally – was losing out to "The Market Economy". Artists and students had to fall back more and more on their own resources. In view of this, the value of the Guild today in supporting its members is well founded and will continue to profit from its artistic legacy.

Besides being a catalogue of all the work in the exhibition, this publication begins with a section on the traditional cultural history of batik, which reaches back 2,000 years. It also clearly explains in illustration and text the modern techniques practised by internationally renowned artists. It is invaluable to any aspiring artist, student or teacher of batik.

Labyrinth
Pat Hodson
90 x 210 cm
Mixed media including batik,
collage and computer imaging

I use wax, dye, silk, paper,
computer, and printer – exploring
a multi-dimensional space where
idea, image, pattern and
construction continually evolve.
Pattern is illusory and real –
within the collage and on the
surface – wax and stitch
– resisting yet interacting with
the digital print.

(photo: M Hodson)

This project would not have been possible without
the help of many people.

The Batik Guild would like to thank:
Heritage Lottery Fund and
The Joan Howes Trust
for their generous contributions.

Our sponsors:
Creative Exhibitions
Art Van Go
Batik in Brighton
Colourcraft
craftynotions.com
Fibrecrafts
Rainbow Silks
Simplee Silk
Textile Techniques
Whaleys of Bradford
Westhope College
The Williamson Museum and Art Gallery, Birkenhead
Gloucester City Museum and Art Gallery
Worthing Art Gallery and Museum
The Museum of East Asian Art, Bath

**Diane Gaffney would like to thank the following for
their valuable contributions to this book:**
Kevin Mead (Art Van Go), Noel Dyrenforth, Robin Paris,
Jane Brunning, Fiona Kerlogue, Leesa Hubbell,
Gasali Adeyemo, Gina Corrigan, Betsy Sterling Benjamin,
Susan McLean, Sarah Tucker, Jill Kennedy,
Hetty van Boekhout, Sue Cowell, Jenn and
Stephen Adamson, Bronwyn Williams-Ellis, Rita Trefois,
Jacques Coenye, Lee Creswell, Rosi Robinson,
Marie-Thérèse King, and Laura Lanceley.

Exhibition design by Jane Brunning.
Photographs by members of The Batik Guild unless
otherwise credited.
Designed by Matt Anderson (07815 195 598).
Printed by Dunnsprint.
Published by The Batik Guild 2006.

ISBN
0-9553817-0-3
978-0-9553817-0-6

Batik on hemp
and cotton by
Bouyei and
Miao people.
(photo: Art Van Go)

CONTENTS

WORLD BATIK   4

INDONESIA
Central Java   5
The North Coast of Java   6
Using batik in Java   9
Sumatra   10
Contemporary Bali batik   11

AFRICA
West Africa   12
Nigeria   13

ASIA AND AUSTRALIA
South-West China   14
Japan   16
India and Sri Lanka   18
Australia   19
Malaysia   19

BATIK TECHNIQUES   20
Cotton   21
Silk   22
Paper   24
Pysanki (batik on eggs)   26
Wood   27
Ceramics   27
Cantings and kystkas   28
Brushes and other tools   30
Stamps and caps   32
Etching or scraffito   33
Using discharges   33
Ro-shibori   34
Starch resist   35
Dyes   36
Teaching children to batik   38

CONTEMPORARY BATIK   40
Useful contacts   62
Places to see batik in the UK   63
Selected books and websites   64

Front cover
Detail of *Adrift*
Noel Dyrenforth
(photo: Art Van Go)

WORLD BATIK

BATIK – A METHOD OF PATTERNING CLOTH WITH WAX AND DYE – GOES BACK THOUSANDS OF YEARS. ALTHOUGH TEXTILE HISTORIANS MAY DISPUTE THE ACTUAL PLACE AND DATE OF ITS ORIGINS, THE EARLIEST FRAGMENTS OF WAX-RESIST CLOTH HAVE BEEN FOUND IN CHINA. IT HAD SPREAD TO JAPAN BY THE EIGHTH CENTURY AND FOUND ITS WAY TO INDIA AND INDONESIA.

Undoubtedly the very finest batik was produced on the island of Java in the nineteenth and early twentieth century. Wonderful batik cloths from Java were brought to Europe by Dutch colonisers and their designs sparked a wave of interest and creativity in the West. Art schools in Eastern and Western Europe and in America explored the technique, and batik production spread through craft workshops and studios. Interest peaked around the 1920s, but waned until the 1960s when batik was taken up again by a new generation.

In homes and workshops in many parts of Asia, batik is still being made on cotton and hemp for use and wear in a tradition which continues to this day.

Batik as a way of making art started in the West in the '60s and spread through the world to countries from Kenya to Sri Lanka. Even in conservative Java, young people from traditional batik-making families saw a new way to sell batik. The wave of young backpackers and later tourists to these areas had a huge impact. In Japan, batik developed in a different way.

The story of batik is a fascinating one: this section will give you a glimpse of it.

1.
Batik workers at a
workshop in Lasem,
Java.
(photo: D. Gaffney)

2.
Hand-drawn cloth from
Solo, Central Java.
(photo: Art Van Go)

3.
Waxing cloth in Cirebon,
Java.
(photo: N. Dyrenforth)

4.
Waxing cloth in Cirebon,
Java.
(photo: N. Dyrenforth)

5.
Making a cap batik in a
workshop in Jogyakarta,
Java.
(photo: D. Gaffney)

BATIK FROM CENTRAL JAVA

Batik is made in many parts of the world but to see some of the very finest batik, you must go to the island of Java, where batik is still made, used, and worn by millions of people every day.

The very word "batik" is Javanese, and it was here that the wax pen or canting (pronounced "chanting") and later the copper stamp or cap (pronounced "chap") were invented, so it is appropriate to start here in batik's "heartland".

Very fine hand-drawn "batik tulis" with its highly refined aesthetic sense and spiritual implications was traditionally an art practised by high-born women. Before beginning a new design, a night of meditation was considered necessary. Designs were imbued with great significance and many reserved for the aristocracy. Batik is still patronised by the Sultans in the Central Javanese towns of Jogyakarta and Solo. In Giriloya a village near the burial grounds of the Jogyakarta court there are just a few women who still know how to make the royal cloths needed for a wedding.

One of them says, "You have to have a perfectly quiet heart and full concentration to do that kind of fine work".

In towns and villages all over Java, men and women make batik in factories, in workshops and in their own back yards. Family batik businesses going back five or six generations still survive in the twenty - first century although they have had to change and adapt to the demands of the market. For example, in the early days the waxing was all done by hand with a canting, and this still continues, but in the 1860s copper stamps were invented. These are used to apply wax and have speeded up the process of making a batik cloth considerably.

In this very conservative society, the vegetable dyes of indigo and soga were exclusively used until the 1960s, but they have now been almost totally replaced by aniline dyes. Both "cap batik" and "batik tulis" are still widely produced and worn in Central Java.

1.
Megamendung.
A design meaning "storm clouds" - is produced by families of Chinese ancestry in Cirebon on Java's northern coast. The same design can be seen in ceramics and embroideries from China.

(photo: Art Van Go)

BATIK FROM THE NORTH COAST OF JAVA

TRADERS, INVADERS, PLANTERS AND COLONISERS CAME TO THE NORTHERN COAST AND EVENTUALLY WERE TO INFLUENCE THE BATIK PRODUCED THERE.

Whilst Central Java was ruled by the Sultans, resulting in a highly conservative society, on the north coast of Java, things were very different.

The Chinese came primarily to trade and later to settle. They brought silk from their homeland and started up batik businesses, which catered for their own needs using their favourite colours and designs.

Several Chinese families still run batik businesses on the north coast including Lina's in Cirebon. Lina comes from five generations of batik makers beginning with her great-great-grandfather who came from China and married a Javanese woman. She still runs the family's business, employing many people in the surrounding villages and selling to Jakarta.

The Dutch were another major influence, having a presence in Indonesia for 400 years

2.
Detail of a sarung produced at Eliza van Zuylen's batik workshop in Pekalongan around 1935. The bouquets of flowers with birds and butterflies are typical of designs created for the Dutch and Indische (Dutch-Indonesian) market.
(photo: Art Van Go)

3.
Detail of a selendang (carrying cloth) Kerek village, Tuban. Hand-spun and woven cotton. Indigo dyed.
(photo: Art Van Go)

4.
Detail of a sarung "Tiga negri" (three countries) a cloth waxed and dyed in three different towns. In earlier times before synthetic dyes were widely available, a batik cloth may have been waxed in Solo, dyed with indigo and soga in Jogyakarta and then sent to Lasem for the final red dye.
(photo: Art Van Go)

5.
Detail of a cloth from Madura With designs of fish scales, and seaweed. Vegetable dyed.
(photo: Art Van Go)

until independence in 1948. Dutch women who came to live in Java envied the cool cotton sarungs worn by Javanese women but wanted something more lively than the typical indigo and brown colours.

Many workshops sprang up at this time producing exquisite hand-drawn batik of very fine quality for Dutch customers. Most of them were run by women, many of Dutch-Indonesian birth, and the batik produced at these workshops became extremely popular. The beautiful colours and floral designs appealed to many, including the Peranakan or Straits Chinese communities in Java, Singapore and Malaysia, and many still wear fine Javanese batik for formal occasions.

On the north coast several towns produced their own unique and individual batik and it is a fascinating quest to find the small workshops which still survive. Lasem, for example, was famous for the red dye produced there. Very distinctive batik is still produced in small villages near Tuban. Cotton is grown in the village, spun and woven on a back strap loom, waxed and then dyed in locally-grown indigo. On the island of Madura, the women of this seafaring community have made their own distinctive batik designs with motifs from the sea for many hundreds of years.

Pekalongan is known as "batik city" where creativity and innovation is positively encouraged and you can order any kind of batik you want! It is also the centre for the production of screen-printed "batik", a cloth very popular throughout South-East Asia.

1.
Shopping in the market.
(photo: D. Gaffney)

2.
Family of the bride
at a wedding in Java.
(photo: D. Gaffney)

3.
Carrying goods in
batik cloths.
(photo: D Gaffney)

4.
The "jamu" lady brings
round her daily medicinal
doses.
(photo: J. Gaffney)

5.
Old lady.
(photo: J. Gaffney)

6.
A dancer in the Royal
Palace (Kraton) in
Jogyakarta, Java.
(photo: N. Dyrenforth)

7.
Baby in a batik selendang
carrying cloth.
(photo: D. Gaffney)

Detail of a kemben
Cap batik from Solo, Central Java
52 x 248 cm
A kemben or breastcloth may be
worn instead of a "kebaya" blouse
for formal and court ceremonies.
(photo: Art Van Go)

USING BATIK IN JAVA

IN JAVA, BATIK IS EVERYWHERE; IN MARKETS AND IN BACK
STREETS THERE IS THE DISTINCTIVE SMELL OF WAX.

Traditional sarungs are still worn by many, especially in rural areas, and even urban babies are carried in a batik sling. Civil servants are encouraged to wear batik shirts by the Indonesian Government's "Batik Fridays" initiative, and design names feature in street names and advertising signs.

The hundreds of patterns each have a name and distinct meaning and they still retain significance. Some are used at events such as a birth, a death and most especially at a wedding. The families will wear batik to show their origins and designs are chosen for their spiritual significance.

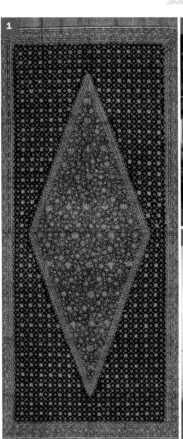

BATIK IN SUMATRA

BATIK IN SUMATRA HAS ITS OWN TRADITIONS AND DISTINCTIVE DESIGNS AND COLOURS.

There is some evidence that batik making was once widespread in Sumatra, and new centres have been established in recent years. The best-known tradition is from Jambi, a region in central Sumatra. In the 1920s Dutch officials produced a report on Jambi batik, and later a curator at the Tropical Institute in Amsterdam produced a series of articles on the subject. At that time most production was in indigo on a ground pre-treated in an infusion of chips from the lembato tree, which produced a yellowish effect in the waxed areas. Sometimes the wax was deliberately cracked and the cloth immersed in an infusion of marelang bark, producing dark brown veining in the yellow. This gave an effect resembling the sparkle of gold.

The 1920s report and articles discussed at length whether or not Jambi also produced batik containing red dyes, finally concluding that indeed this was the case. Some examples of hand-waxed Jambi cloths from this period containing red are held in Dutch and British museums. Some older cloths containing red from Jambi have patterns produced by stamping on a resist or by stencilling.

Jambi designs typically consist of symmetrically arranged rows of discrete motifs, usually of flower shapes, themselves symmetrical, which distinguishes them from Javanese batik. These designs correspond with the motifs found in the gold thread brocade, or songket, produced in east coast Sumatran centres including Jambi.

Batik production continues today, generally using a wider palette of artificial dyes, though some producers still use natural dyestuffs.

S#A103 #119 Vintage
S#B230 #169 Prussian
S#B231 #169 Pr
S#B233 #169 Prussian
S#B231 #36 Amber
S#B230 #128 Midnight
S#B224 #169 Prussian
S#B233 #36 Amber

CONTEMPORARY BALI BATIK

SEVERAL HUNDRED YEARS OF JAVANESE BATIK-MAKING EXPERTISE AND THE WELCOMING BALINESE CULTURE AND LANDSCAPE SEDUCED MANY TOURISTS IN THE 60'S TO RELOCATE AND HITCH THEIR RESOURCES TO THE DEVELOPMENT OF A NEW FORM OF BATIK FOR A WESTERN MARKETPLACE.

"Bali batik" is a multi-cultural, international style that began to appear on tourist items, such as T-shirts and pareo beach wraps, in the late 1970s. In order to support a Bali-based (usually surfing) lifestyle, entrepreneurial travellers from developed countries started collaborating with the batik cap (copper stamp) artisans and dyers of Java to create batik fashion products for export to Western markets. Having little in common with the aristocratic and mysticism-infused batik of the Javanese courts, this innovative cloth is patterned with multiple layers of free-form cap stamping and background dye effects – such as marbleising, tie-dye, and the multi-coloured mottled texture achieved by splattering colour on smocked or scrunched base cloth with brushes or squeeze bottles. Quilters and crafters worldwide began collecting "Balis" in the early 1990s and continue to support the production of thousands of metres of this remarkably complex, hand-made cloth each year.

Five examples of
wax print from ABC.
(photo: Art Van Go)

Wax print at a West African Market
(photo: M. Relph)

WAX RESIST FROM WEST AFRICA

THE CLOTH USED MOST OFTEN FOR DRESSES, WRAPPERS AND HEAD CLOTHS THROUGHOUT
SUB-SAHARAN AFRICA, IS LIKELY TO BE A KIND OF BATIK KNOWN AS "WAX PRINT". THE STORY
BEHIND THIS COLOURFUL AND FLAMBOYANT FABRIC IS A FASCINATING TALE

The development of wax print began in the nineteenth century as an attempt by Dutch textile manufacturers to produce cheap batik through mechanisation, and then to sell it back to their Indonesian colony.

A machine for printing banknotes was adapted to apply a waxy pine resin on to cotton. However, this produced a "crackle", which Indonesian customers rejected as a sign of inferior craftsmanship. Dutch manufacturers took the cloth to their trading posts on the Gold Coast (in what is now Ghana) in the hope of finding a market.

The popularity of wax print cloth spread swiftly and within a few years, factories in several parts of Europe including the textile centre of Manchester had started to produce it. Today only two remain: ABC (Brunnschweiler) in Cheshire and Vlissco in Holland. The once numerous smaller firms eventually closed down and in many cases sold their machinery to producers in Africa. Many of these still operate and wax print remains the most widely distributed cloth in Africa. European-produced wax print still carries a premium and is preferred to locally produced cloth, but Chinese-made wax print and "fancy print" (imitation

wax) have recently started to make their way on to the market.

Wax print has been made at Brunnschweiler's since 1908. The company has recently been taken over by a Chinese textile firm, interested in its fascinating archive of designs and the strong brand name of ABC. The earliest designs show distinct Javanese influences, and many are still reproduced. Some designs depict well-known proverbs, many give a strong sense of local history and commemorate important events – originally perhaps a wedding or the funeral of an important chief, but also the opening of the Guinness factory in Lagos! Political leaders have seen the potential propaganda value in wax print designs and at election time, cloth featuring slogans, symbols or pictures of leaders may be given away.

The story of African wax printed cloth is a fascinating footnote in the great traditions of world batik. Its origins may be in colonial exploitation and ruthless trade, but its development since, with the many clear local preferences for designs and colours, means that it has become a true symbol of national identity.

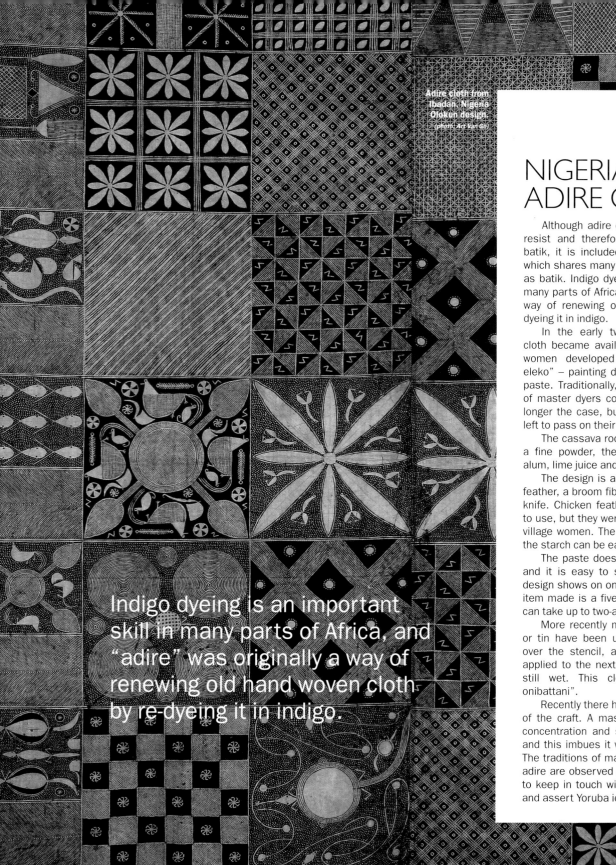

Adire cloth from Ibadan, Nigeria. Olokun design.
(photo: Art Van Go)

NIGERIAN ADIRE CLOTH

Although adire cloth is made with a starch resist and therefore is not strictly speaking batik, it is included here as a resist method which shares many of the same characteristics as batik. Indigo dyeing is an important skill in many parts of Africa, and adire was originally a way of renewing old hand-woven cloth by re-dyeing it in indigo.

In the early twentieth century, imported cloth became available in Nigeria and Yoruba women developed the technique of "adire eleko" – painting designs with cassava starch paste. Traditionally, only women from a family of master dyers could make adire. This is no longer the case, but there are now only a few left to pass on their skills.

The cassava root is dried and pounded into a fine powder, then made into a paste with alum, lime juice and a little sulphur.

The design is applied using a chicken wing feather, a broom fibre or a small wedge-shaped knife. Chicken feathers are painstakingly slow to use, but they were the only tools available to village women. The cloth is dyed in indigo and the starch can be easily removed by soaking it.

The paste does not penetrate to the back, and it is easy to spot an adire cloth as the design shows on only one side. The most usual item made is a five-yard wrapper (4.6m) which can take up to two-and-a-half years to complete.

More recently metal stencils cut from zinc or tin have been used. The paste is applied over the stencil, and the stencil moved and applied to the next section while the paste is still wet. This cloth is known as "adire onibattani".

Recently there has been a conscious revival of the craft. A master dyer pours great time, concentration and spiritual effort into a cloth and this imbues it with value and significance. The traditions of making and wearing authentic adire are observed as a way for Yoruba people to keep in touch with their cultural inheritance and assert Yoruba identity.

Indigo dyeing is an important skill in many parts of Africa, and "adire" was originally a way of renewing old hand woven cloth by re-dyeing it in indigo.

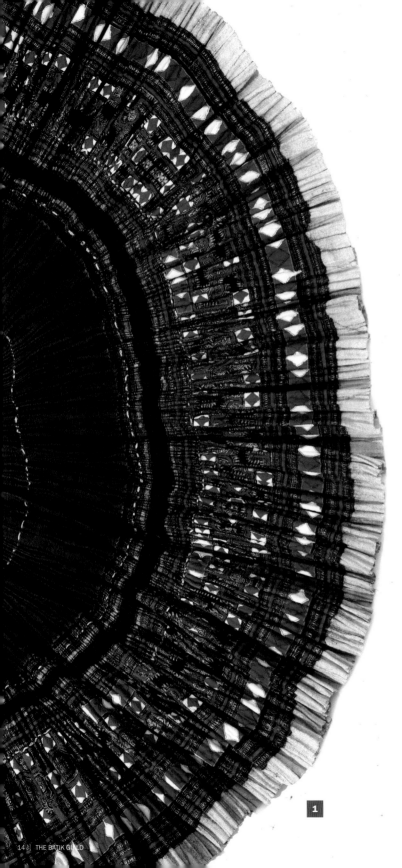

1.
Hemp batik skirt
embellished with
appliqué and
embroidery.
Miao people,
Vietnam.
(photo: Art Van Go)

SOUTH-WEST CHINA

ORIGINATING IN SOUTH-WEST CHINA, HILLTRIBE WOMEN
IN LAOS, THAILAND, AND VIETNAM CONTINUE THEIR BATIK-
MAKING TRADITIONS.

In southern China batik has been found which dates back to the Han
dynasty around 2,000 years ago. There are about 60 ethnic minorities in
China and the Miao, the Gejia (a sub-group of the Miao) and the Bouyei,
make their own highly individual batik. Around nine million Miao people
live in the provinces of Guizhou and Yunnan in the South-West. In the early
nineteenth century, some Miao migrated into Vietnam, Laos and Northern
Thailand where they are now known as H'mong.

The Miao, Gejia and the Bouyei people have always been self-
sufficient, following their own patterns of life and agriculture, marrying
amongst themselves and preserving their own customs and arts. The
most common means of expressing identity, family wealth and artistic
creativity is through the adornment of jewellery and clothing. There are
numerous festivals where everyone wears very finely embroidered and
batiked costumes. Girls start learning to embroider and produce batik
from the age of six or seven years and spend hundreds of hours
producing their costumes. Nowadays many go to school and may leave
the village for work. They have less time to learn the traditional skills, and
find traditional costumes inconvenient for everyday wear, so it is becoming
common to see them only at festival times.

Geometric designs are drawn on to cotton or hemp with small
triangular tools made by the village blacksmith. The beeswax is heated in
a little pot, resting in hot embers. The designs are drawn from the natural
world around them, although many of these names and meanings are
now lost. The dye is traditionally a natural indigo made from a paste of
harvested plants soaked in wooden barrels. It can take up to 25 days to
achieve the dark rich blue colour by dipping every day. Nowadays
synthetic indigo as well as other aniline dyes may be used.

Jacket sleeves, skirt panels, apron fronts and baby carriers are most
commonly batiked. The batik is used as a base decoration, which may in
some cases be almost hidden by the extravagance of embroidery and
appliqué. The finely-pleated skirts are wonderful creations – usually made
of lengths of as much as eight metres of hand-woven hemp or cotton
batik decorated with bands of cross-stitch, and appliqué. There are many
ways of forming the permanent pleats including starching and steaming.

1

2.
A H'mong village in North Thailand with indigo dyed hemp strips hanging outside.
(photo: D. Gaffney)

3.
Freshly dyed indigo skirt panels drying outside a house in North Thailand.
(photo: D. Gaffney)

4.
Batiking on hemp.
(photo: D. Gaffney)

5.
The hemp strip is laid onto a board and the wax melted in a little pot kept in the fire embers.
(photo: D. Gaffney)

6.
Bouyei batik.
Detail of a baby carrier, a waxed piece and the tools used to apply the wax.
(photo: Art Van Go)

7.
Bouyei girls washing their indigo batik at the river.
(photo: N. Dyrenforth)

8.
This wax tool has two spouts and is used for drawing parallel lines.
(photo: D. Gaffney)

The artist Katsuji Yamade with one of his award-winning kimonos.
(photo: L. Creswell)

ROZOME FROM JAPAN

A WAX RESIST TECHNIQUE WHICH HAS ITS ROOTS IN THE EIGHTH CENTURY HAS BEEN REVIVED.

Kisakata Lagoon
Katsuji Yamade
Silk kimono
167 x 137 cm

This kimono was inspired by a haiku by Basho, a poet well known in Japan. When Basho visited Kisakata, he saw thousands of islands in the lagoon. But after an earthquake, the scene was totally changed, and the lagoon is a field now. I imagined how the scene might have looked from Basho's haiku and recreated it on this kimono.
(photo: Happoh-do Co.)

Rozome (meaning "wax dyeing") is a Japanese batik process that first appeared more than 1,200 years ago. The vibrant rozome of contemporary Japan is an outgrowth of an eighth-century textile patterning technique, which was rediscovered in the last century as a dynamic painterly process. Rozome is one of the four resist processes now practised in Japan to decorate the beautiful kimono. However, it is the use of rozome as contemporary art, presented as four- or six-panel folding screens and huge three-metre paintings, that is most noteworthy. Rozome artists are seen as the true "painters" of the Japanese textile world.

Many artists who work with rozome base their artistic inspiration on nature. Trained in observing the world around them, they turn to this subject for poetic and decorative imagery in their work. The use of empty space is an additional composition element.

The artists have a strong interest in colour, design, composition and painterly styles. They rely primarily on the brush to apply the wax; however, some artists have expanded wax-application techniques to include stencilling, stamping, etching and rolling wax for textural effects. While rozome and traditional batik have many things in common, rozome differs in a number of specific ways. The brush is used in rozome for both wax as well as dye application producing a fine controlled technique. The white line of the Indonesian canting tool and repeat patterns of the cap stamp are rare. When applying colour the Japanese prefer the shaded luminosity possible with brush-applied dye in contrast to the flat, saturated colour of Indonesian dip-dye technique.

Western batik artists are delighted to have this '"new" Asian source of inspiration. In Japan, rozome is accepted as fine art and respected as a valid technique for contemporary art. It is a pleasure to see rozome receiving the recognition and exposure it deserves throughout the world.

Snowy Heron in Lotus Pond
Yusuke Tange
175 x 150 cm
(photo: Y. Tange)

Tiger
Wax resist on cotton
from the workshop of
Mahinda Ranaweera,
Kandy, Sri Lanka.
(photo: D. Gaffney)

INDIA AND SRI LANKA

THERE IS A LONG TRADITION OF USING RESISTS TO DECORATE TEXTILES IN INDIA. IT IS BELIEVED THAT RESIST METHODS WITH RICE STARCH, WAX AND MORDANTS WERE USED AS EARLY AS THE FIRST CENTURY AD.

The batik industry was at its peak in the seventeenth and eighteenth centuries when batik textiles were exported to many parts of the world, including Europe, Persia and Java. The traditional method was to combine batik with direct dye painting with a "kalam" pen. Many of the motifs and designs seen in Javanese batik come from India and their names are derived from Hindi.

Batik, however, declined sharply in India as it was seen as a time-consuming process, and was largely replaced by block printing. There has been a more recent revival of batik and it is now once again used to make art and to decorate fabrics.

Batik was introduced into Sri Lanka in the 1960s and it is still widely made by hand. Most of the arts including painting, sculpture and architecture in Sri Lanka, are inspired by its long and lasting Buddhist tradition, and batik paintings are no different.

Sri Lankan batik has developed into its own unique style based on traditional religious themes and the natural world. However, a need to sell to the growing tourism industry has meant that a wide variety of subjects are portrayed. Some of the best and most original batik paintings are made in Kandy.

AUSTRALIA

INDIGENOUS BATIK ARTISTS ARE
NOW REPRESENTED IN STATE AND
NATIONAL COLLECTIONS IN AUSTRALIA
AND OVERSEAS.

Australian batik has, on occasion, been enriched by its Asia-Pacific proximity, but the most significant batik practice in Australia takes place in remote central and western desert regions and is made by Aboriginal women. Ernabella is home to approximately 400 Pitjantjatjara people and lies 440 km south-west of Alice Springs. It was here that batik was first introduced to the indigenous people of Australia in 1971.

Ernabella batiks are often a combination of "Walka" the Pitjantjatjara word that translates as "meaningful mark". This one word has to do service for the entire Western vocabulary of art, since the terms and concepts of art, decoration and artist do not exist in Pitjantjatjara. The vast visual vocabulary of traditional mark making is the basis on which all contemporary visual expression, including batik, rests.

These iconographic markings always signify something important. They may be marks which originate from the artist's environment, plants or animal tracks, they may have reference to ancient sand drawings, ceremonial body painting, the patterns on a bird's wing or goanna skin, or they may signify one small part of a larger ancient story.

More often than not, artworks depict "country". There may be representations of everyday life – collecting bush foods, the availability of water, or seasonal changes in the landscape. The significance, however, may also be far more complex, and non-indigenous viewers will only ever receive a modified version.

Alison Carroll, senior batik artist at Ernabella, with a piece of her work.

Pitjantjatjara women Alison Carroll and Nyukana Baker are active and respected senior batik artists at Ernabella Arts. Their wax resist and dyed silk lengths of up to four metres have become world famous.
(photo: S. Mclean)

MALAYSIA

MALAYSIA'S TRADITION OF BATIK-MAKING HAS BEEN REVIVED
AND IS BEING PROMOTED FOR THE FASHION MARKET.

Javanese batik has been imported into Malaysia since the fourteenth century and is still worn. Fine hand-drawn floral batik from Pekalongan remains popular with Nonya women of the Straits Chinese communities in Malacca and Penang who traditionally wear a batik sarung with a finely embroidered kebaya jacket.

An independent batik cottage industry started around a hundred years ago and centred on the east coast states of Trengganu and Kelantan. Traditionally Malay batik uses wooden block prints or brushes rather than caps and cantings. The motifs depict the natural world particularly sea creatures such as shrimps and fish. There are still around 120 batik producers in Kelantan.

When Malaysia gained independence in 1957, batik was seen as a part of its cultural heritage and its use was encouraged. But interest had dwindled until 2003 when the Prime Minister's wife headed a programme of promotion aimed at revitalising Malaysian batik for the fashion market. Some exciting and innovative contemporary batik fashions are now being produced. A huge amount of genuine and printed batik is sold throughout South-East Asia and Malaysia is intent on positioning itself as the market leader.

1.
A gamelan orchestra in Kuala Lumpur with batik designs featured.
(photo: D. Gaffney)

2.
Entries in the annual batik fashion competition held in Kuala Lumpur, Malaysia, to encourage contemporary batik production.
(photo: D. Gaffney)

Estuary
Sarah Tucker
Batik on cotton
84 x 102 cm
(photo: Art Van Go)

BATIK
TECHNIQUES

BATIK IS HISTORICALLY THE MOST EXPRESSIVE AND
SUBTLE OF THE RESIST METHODS. THE FOLLOWING PAGES
SHOW A FEW OF THE MANY WAYS YOU CAN EXPERIMENT
WITH THE BASIC MATERIALS OF WAX AND DYE.

Making batik may be technically demanding but it is also extremely satisfying. It draws people from a scientific background intrigued by its chemistry as well as those from an artistic background who enjoy batik's uniquely tactile and fluid qualities. Many love the sense of surprise, which is always a part of the batik process no matter how experienced the artist.

This section will give you an insight into some of the many ingenious techniques used in batik. There are many surfaces that can take wax and dye. Cotton is the most common, but as you will see, batik is also successful on silk, paper, wood, leather and ceramics. Wax can be applied with all kinds of tools and some are shown here, but there are many more. The dyes are also many and varied as are the ways they can be used. The most important thing is to experiment and to enjoy the process as well as the result.

"Batik for me means colour and change. This is one of the reasons I find seascapes so particularly satisfying. There are constant shifts of reflected light which have somehow to be conveyed in the finished batik."

Sarah Tucker

BATIK ON COTTON

COTTON IS THE FABRIC MOST COMMONLY USED IN BATIK. IT IS STRONG AND VERSATILE AND LENDS ITSELF TO MANY DIFFERENT PROCESSES.

After initial pencil drawing on white cotton lawn I use tiny cantings and small bristle brushes to wax the highlights, to catch the sparkle. I often use a kystka, a tool used for waxing eggs. This tool is perfect for tiny dots and fine lines. I then wash Procion® dyes across the fabric starting with the very palest of shades. As in water-colour processes, wet on wet, I damp the fabric first with the fixative to enable the dyes to blend.

The images are then slowly built up with successive waxing and dyeing. The spaces left between the waxed areas are as important as the areas waxed. Although I hand-paint regularly, dip-dyeing is crucial to my work. It means that the colours are constantly changed, muted and transmuted by the immediacy of the dye bath.

As the work progresses, I often choose to boil the fabric. This removes all the wax and gives me the chance to rethink the colours and add variety of texture by over-waxing and over-dyeing. The result, I hope, has something of the fluidity of water. The process is one of serendipity, of never knowing exactly how colours will react one with another, and how the waxed areas will crack.

Finally, the whole fabric is covered in wax except for the lines I have left around shapes which, when dyed in the last colour, will help to add depth and definition.

Sarah Tucker

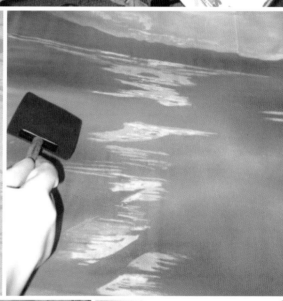

"I use all types of silk from the very finest mousselines and chiffons to the heaviest crêpes and doupions. In fact whereas there may be problems with the thicker silks when using gutta, wax penetrates very thick silks, even silk velvet."

Jill Kennedy

BATIK ON SILK

WAX CAN BE USED AS A RESIST ON SILK AS WELL AS THE MORE USUAL COTTON.

The wax can be applied using all kinds of tools such as brushes, cantings, kystkas, sponges, sticks, corks, homemade printing blocks, metal forks, cotton buds, rags, scrubbing brushes, or stencils.

Both paraffin and beeswax can be used, and altering the mix of paraffin and beeswax in the wax pot can create different wax effects. For a smooth effect with no crackling use more beeswax but add more paraffin wax for the traditional crackle look. If the wax will not adhere to the silk more beeswax may be needed. The usual temperature for the wax is around 48°C, not so hot for the very fine silks and a little hotter for silk crêpes and velvets.

Using the direct painting method means a huge variety of colours can be produced on silk. As silk dyes are transparent the colours produced and the colour combinations are endless.

You can produce interesting textural effects by adding salt (coarse rock or fine table). Preserving sugar can also be applied to the wet silk dyes to move the pigments of the dyes before they have been fixed into the fabric.

Bleach cannot be used on silk, as it will develop holes, but these can, of course, produce another interesting texture. However, discharge paste or alcohol, such as ethyl alcohol, or surgical spirit can be used to remove colour. Beware, if too much alcohol is used it will start to eat into the wax.

Remove the silk from the frame and iron between sheets of absorbent paper to remove most of the wax.

If steam-fix silk dyes have been used the silk must be steamed to fix the dyes permanently into the silk. After fixing it is usually necessary to remove the final traces of wax in white spirit or to send your finished piece to the dry-cleaners.

Jill Kennedy

Come Shine
Jill Kennedy
Batik on silk
90 x 90 cm

"Come Shine" was inspired by a rainy day in Hong Kong full of umbrellas followed by a very sunny day in Singapore. It is painted on crêpe de Chine no. 12 with wax, kystkas and wax brushes using steam-fix silk dyes.
(photo: Art Van Go)

1.
Applying dye with a brush.

2.
Applying wax with a fine canting.

3.
Silk batik – wax applied with a canting.

4.
Wax applied with a sponge.

5.
The wax can be cracked before the final dye to give the characteristic crackle effect.

The Final Journey
Lee Creswell
Batik on silk
53 x 71 cm

I have always liked to see the movement of water; be it a babbling brook, soft waves lapping on the shores or, in this case, a waterfall. Before going to spawn the salmon has to swim upstream against the force of the showering waterfall and I wanted to capture the energy of the salmon as it leaps upwards against the waters in its determination to reach its destination.

BATIK
ON PAPER

"You can use any kind of paper which absorbs dye. Just experiment for yourself. Batik on paper has a number of advantages. It is cheap and a frame for stretching is not necessary. Don't use expensive watercolour-paper or handmade paper. Batik on paper is versatile. It can be used for a variety of purposes with a personal touch: framed on the wall or used as a book-cover, folder, greetings card, lampshade, gift-wrapping paper etc. Nothing is wasted."

Hetty van Boekhout

Found Object I and II
Hetty van Boekhout
Wax, dye, bleach,
collage on paper
54 x 40 cm each

With batik on paper
I discovered new
possibilities which
I constantly explore.
Paper has its own tactile
qualities and properties,
thick or thin, rough or
smooth, opaque or
transparent.

(photo: Art Van Go)

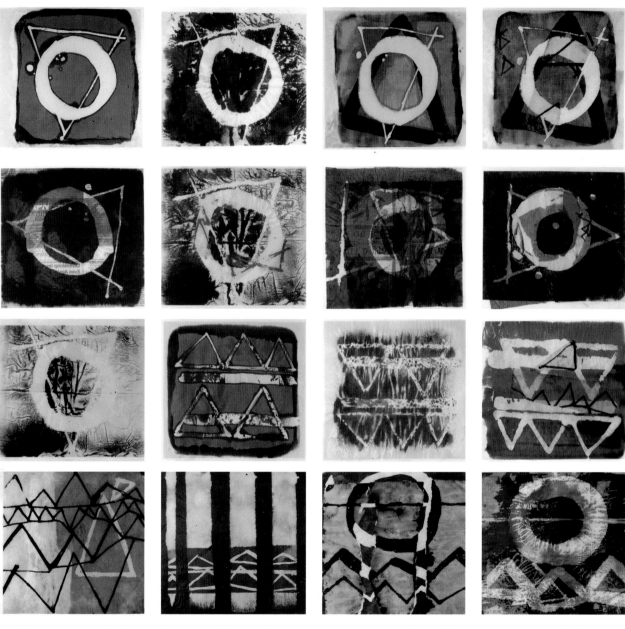

Always put a sheet of paper, like newsprint, under the paper you are going to work on. This is your base paper. Don't remove your work from the base till it is finished and ironed. You might get an unexpected surprise print from your original work on it, which can be used as a starting point for a new work, adding collage etc. Handle papers with care while wet. It is not necessary to rinse bleach with water. Use pure bleach or diluted bleach for shades of tone. Waxed tissue paper becomes transparent when ironed and works well for collage. You can iron pieces of tissue paper on top of your work. Shapes can be moved around. The idea has a better chance of being developed without being forced. Collage creates layers of skin. Transparent papers create depth, overlapping each other. For a long-lasting result it is best to dye coloured tissue papers before using. Some tissue papers fade after a while.
Hetty van Boekhout

PYSANKI - BATIK ON EGGS

A TRADITION FROM POLAND AND THE UKRAINE

Basket of eggs
Sue Cowell

Whilst on a teacher exchange programme in Canada some years ago, I became fascinated by the Ukrainian art of decorating eggs using wax and dyes. Since then I have specialised in the technique sometimes following traditional Ukrainian designs but also creating more contemporary designs particularly in the Art Nouveau style.

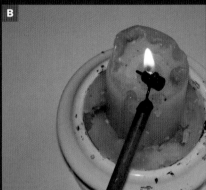

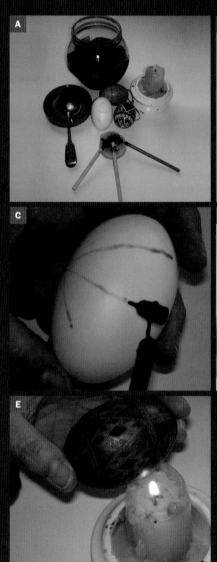

A. All you need is a candle, a lump of beeswax, some vegetable dyes and a drawing tool called a 'kystka'.

B. The kystka is heated by moving it backwards and forwards through the candle flame, thus melting the beeswax inside the kystka.

C. As the melted wax flows, lines can be drawn on to the egg (preferably white) just like drawing with a pen.

D. The egg is put into a jar of dye by lowering it into the dye on a spoon. The egg stays in the dye for about five minutes. It can then be taken out, mopped dry with paper towel and waxing can continue straight away.

E. After a succession of waxings and dyeings in different colour dyes, the wax is removed by holding the egg in the flame of the candle and rubbing off the melted wax with a paper towel. Finally a paper towel soaked in white spirit will remove the last residues of wax.

The decorated eggs should be covered with several coats of varnish. They can be blown to use as

Mahogany Bowl
Jenn and Stephen Adamson
Batik on wood
21 x 7.5 cm
Driftwood from a Sussex beach and
procion© dyes.

BATIK ON CERAMICS

The wax-resist process on ceramics and tiles known as "cuerda seca" (dry cord) goes back to the Babylonian empire of 600 BC. From the fourteenth century on it was widely used in Spain and the Arabic world.

Hot wax and ground manganese dioxide are drawn directly on to the unglazed fired tile. Glazes are then applied by brush. The wax-manganese lines create a resistant barrier to the glaze allowing different coloured glazes to be used alongside each other. At the end of the firing, the manganese remains as a dark line, the wax having burnt off.

BATIK ON WOOD

It is possible to use most batik techniques on wood and veneers with care and some modifications. We advise you to dry the wood naturally because drying it quickly could cause splitting especially with veneers. When waxing it is helpful to have the wax a little hotter than for fabric to allow a smoother flow. Lighter coloured woods like pine allow good colour take up, but darker woods such as beech, elm, yew produce some curious colours. The grain effects are always fascinating.

Apply fibre-reactive dyes slowly and carefully, as the dye takes longer to penetrate the wood and can slide around the surface.

The best way to remove the final wax on curved surfaces is with a high temperature blowtorch, with two people working together for safety. To finish apply several layers of French polish to the surface, although other finishes could be experimented with.

The shapes and combinations of wood and veneer are taking batik into another dimension, which has not yet been fully explored.

Jenn Adamson

Three stages on the way to the finished bowl.

Quicksplash
Bronwyn Williams-Ellis
Ceramic tile
28 x 23 cm

Having seen the possibilities of using wax on ceramics in the Alhambra museum, in the early 1980s, I worked on a practical way to recreate and reintroduce the process helped by the realisation that batik on textiles was a parallel process which also provided suitable tools and materials! To me, tiles are inherently static and the contrast of this bold fluid line is important. In my work the actual line is visually significant in its own right, carrying the life and energy of the drawing right through to the finished piece rather than merely acting as a physical barrier.

(photo: P. O'Connor)

1.
Anne Bologna
using a kystka.
(photo: E. O'Sullivan)

2.
Wipe off any
excess wax.

3.
Noel Dyrenforth
using a canting.
(photo: M. Wicks)

4.
A canting can
even be used with
a ruler.

5.
A fine canting
is used for small
dots and fine lines.
(photo: M. Hodson)

6.
A wider spouted
canting is used for
thick lines and to
fill in large areas.
(photo: M. Hodson)

CANTINGS AND KYSTKAS

All kinds of tools can be used to apply wax in batik. The amazing fineness of the batik of Java would not have been possible without the invention of the canting. The canting gives the artist a far greater degree of control than a brush and it is still widely used. The copper bowl is designed to keep the wax hot and flowing for as long as possible. The size of the spout varies and this controls the thickness of the line. There have been all kinds of variations and modifications on the design, and in Java cantings with as many as seven or eight spouts are used regularly.

In Eastern Europe, the tool used for waxing on to eggs is the kystka and many artists like the tiny dots and fine lines it produces.

K7 in Movement
Rita Trefois
Batik collage on cotton
90 x 110 cm

A batik painter and
lecturer, I trained in textile
chemistry and decorative
art. I have 30 years'
experience in this field
and am passionate about
the batik technique.
A background of scientific
and artistic education
encourages the conflict
between technical skill
and free creativity.
Somewhere in the middle
between technique and
inspiration, a field of
tension exists where
my art works prosper.
(photo: R. Trefois)

Red Bamboo
Jane Dwight
Batik on paper
53 x 114 cm

I am a Chinese Brush painter and use old Chinese brushes to apply the wax. "*Red Bamboo*" was made using table napkins and newsprint, printing and painting with wax with a Chinese brush and red dyes.

(photo Art Van Go)

Some of the variety of tools that can be used to apply wax.

"The variety of drawing materials which can be used for the hot liquid wax is infinite. All have their own characteristics through which a specific structure arises."

Jacques Coenye

BRUSHES AND OTHER TOOLS

ALL KINDS OF BRUSHES CAN BE USED.

 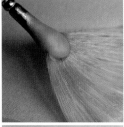  

  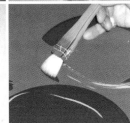

Devon Landscape I
Jacques Coenye
Batik on cotton
99 x 84 cm

I find inspiration for my work in nature and in my imagination. Nature gives images which are constantly in motion and liable to change. The first morning light which slides over an object lets us observe this in a unique moment which constantly changes through the intensity and position of the light and colour temperature. For me the landscape of Devon is an inexhaustible source of inspiration. The light on the sloping plains and granite can be gentle and hard. The forms that arise are in continuous movement. Somewhere there is a moment that can be frozen for the creation of colours and forms.

(photo: J. Coenye)

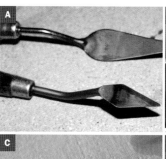

USING A PALETTE KNIFE

A.
A small palette knife can be used to melt the wax on cotton.

B.
The knife is heated up in a flame, but don't let it get too hot.

C.
The knife can be rubbed over the wax and will melt it.

D.
This gives a more transparent texture to the wax.

1. 2.
Making and using
home-made wire
stamps.

1. 2.
Making and using
home-made wire
stamps.

3.
A Javanese cap
and waxed cloth

4. 5.
Using a
Javanese cap.

6.
Copper stamps are
made by trained
craftsmen. The
work calls for
patience and great
accuracy and
unfortunately the
number of men who
can still make these
small works of art
is diminishing
every year.

7.
Potato mashers
make great
stamps for wax.

STAMPS AND CAPS

ALL KINDS OF METAL STAMPS CAN BE USED TO MAKE REPEAT PATTERNS.

In Java, copper stamps were first introduced and used in the 1860s – an extension of an earlier use of wooden blocks. The use of these caps saved the Javanese batik industry when the Dutch attempted to mechanise the batik process. They are still widely used to make "cap batik" – cloth where the wax has been applied by stamp rather than canting. Copper is the best material as it retains the heat so well, but there are many good substitutes – you can make your own stamps from wire, use potato mashers, cookie cutters and even woodblocks.

USING A COPPER STAMP

You will need a flat-bottomed pan wide enough to take the stamp. Put a pan scourer or a pad of cotton in the bottom and heat the wax. The stamp will also need to get hot so leave it in the wax for 10 - 15 minutes before its ready to use. Put your cloth or paper on to a few newspapers to give some padding and then use the stamp rocking it from back to front. You will need to experiment to get the temperature of the wax and the stamp right but once it is going well, you will find you can print many repeats or a whole length of cloth quite quickly.

Noel Dyrenforth pioneered modern batik innovation in the 1960s by exploring new techniques. The etching and discharge processes in particular, opened a whole new perspective on batik.

Noel Dyrenforth
(photo: Art Van Go)

USING BLEACH OR DISCHARGE

Using discharges to take out colour can be used on cotton, silk or paper. Experiments will show that different dyes and surfaces will react to bleach with very interesting results.

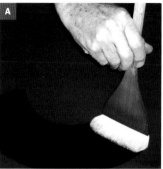

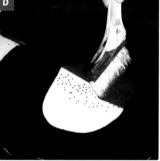
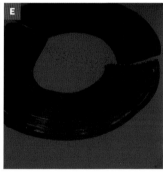

A. The blue shape is reserved with wax. Refill the brush regularly for an even penetration of hot wax into the fabric. Check the back of the cloth to make sure it has been completely covered.

B. Fine dots of wax are applied with a canting.

C. Having waxed over the blue image, the unwaxed area is painted with a discharge solution to remove the colour. Thin household bleach can be used diluted with 50% water. Take care and use rubber gloves and protective glasses. Here the bleach is already starting to take effect.

D. When the bleach has taken effect, wash it out thoroughly with cold water, dry and apply colour again.

E. The finished result shows the invasive qualities of the bleach into the wax. Sensitive waxing can create tonal and textural interest.

ETCHING OR SCRAFFITO IN WAX

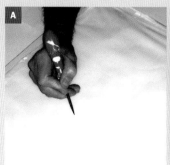
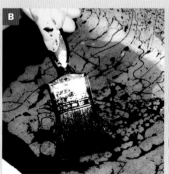
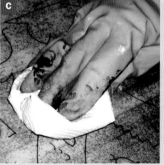
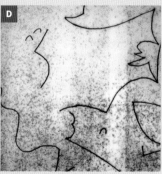

A. Draw or trace a design on to the fabric, and then brush an even amount of wax over the whole area. Remove the cloth from the frame and put it on to a hard plastic or glass surface. Inscribe firmly into the fabric using a tool with a dull metal point (so as not to tear the fabric). Interest can be added by cracking the wax.

B. The etched line exposes the cloth to the action of the dye when it is put into a dye bath. Brushing helps penetration.

C. After dip-dyeing, the surface is cleaned, dried and the wax removed.

D. The line revealed can be as precise and fresh as a pencil drawing.

RO-SHIBORI

A RESIST TECHNIQUE FROM JAPAN

Shibori is the Japanese art of manipulating or compressing the fabric by folding, turning, twisting or sewing cloth, thus resisting the penetration of dyes. Patterns are formed by any one of these principles. The word "ro" is the Japanese word for "wax". There are many different ro-shibori techniques. The example below shows one of them.

It is recommended that the fabric is washed and ironed out before stitching. Silk should be pre-washed in lukewarm water with a wool detergent with 1-2 teaspoonfuls of Calgon if the water is hard. By washing the fabric, any finish will be removed and it will take the dye more easily.

Always plan your design and calculate the length of the repeat patterns, if any, before cutting the fabric or stitching it.

Lee Creswell

Detail of tunic
Lee Creswell
Ro-shibori on silk

This outfit shows two different shibori techniques. The floret pattern is karamatsu ro-shibori as described below. The florets dominate the short front bodice whilst the central panel of the long back shows the bark structure of the mokume shibori technique.

(photo: P. Mennim)

Shibat Hexa
Karla de Ketaelare
Ro-shibori on silk
40 x 250 cm each

Drawing together traditions is a way of working. Mingle age-old techniques for them to crystallise into something new that has always been there. Shibats (a combination of shibori and batik) tend to be like that. Faithful to what precedes them.

(photo: Art Van Go)

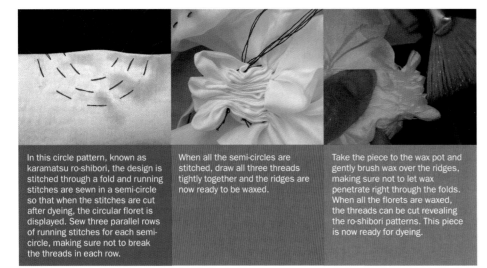

In this circle pattern, known as karamatsu ro-shibori, the design is stitched through a fold and running stitches are sewn in a semi-circle so that when the stitches are cut after dyeing, the circular floret is displayed. Sew three parallel rows of running stitches for each semi-circle, making sure not to break the threads in each row.

When all the semi-circles are stitched, draw all three threads tightly together and the ridges are now ready to be waxed.

Take the piece to the wax pot and gently brush wax over the ridges, making sure not to let wax penetrate right through the folds. When all the florets are waxed, the threads can be cut revealing the ro-shibori patterns. This piece is now ready for dyeing.

ADIRE ELEKO

A STARCH-RESIST TECHNIQUE FROM NIGERIA

In Nigeria among the Yoruba people, a kind of batik is made called adire eleko. The resist is not wax, but a paste made from cassava flour. Cassava is a root like a sweet potato, which is dried and pounded into a fine flour, then mixed with water and lime juice. You may be able to buy cassava flour or you can try mixing corn or wheat flour to a smooth, thick paste.

1.
Gasali Adeyemo, a batik artist from Nigeria mixing cassava paste.

2.
Detail of an adire cloth from Nigeria. Starch resist and indigo dye.
(photo: Art Van Go)

A.
For truly authentic adire, the paste is applied using a chicken wing feather, but you can substitute a paintbrush. Most designs are geometric using straight lines and circles. It is said that the feather from the right side of the chicken will make the best clockwise circles.

B.
The paste should be put on thickly and then allowed to thoroughly dry out. This may need to be left overnight. The fabric will shrink slightly as the paste dries.

C.
Traditionally adire is dyed using indigo. As the paste will dissolve if left too long in the dye, it should be left in the dye for only a minute or two.

D.
Each time it is dyed it needs to have time to oxidise (change in colour from green to blue) and dry before being dipped in the indigo again. Usually the indigo is applied four or five times until the required depth of colour is achieved.

E.
Once the fabric is dry, the paste can be scraped off easily with a knife. The resist leaves a pale blue rather than white.

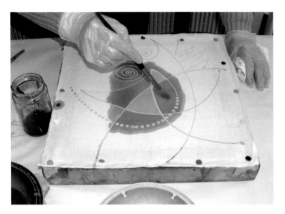

Amy in Turquoise
Marina Elphick
Batik on cotton satin
75 x 75 cm

My batiks are worked with brushes
and cantings and dyed using both
the traditional dip-dye bath and
hand-painting. I work on heavy
cotton satin, which enables me to
build up delicate variations of tone,
using multiple layers of wax, as well
as achieving strong, saturated
colours. I enjoy the immediacy of the
dyeing process and the intense,
vibrant hues that are created,
allowing the final crackle to "dance"
life and resonance into the batik.
This is a portrait of my daughter and
her world of dreams at the
age of twelve.

DYES

FIBRE-REACTIVE DYES ARE IDEAL TO USE WITH BATIK AS THEY WORK WELL IN COLD WATER.
THEY CAN BE USED AS DIP DYES OR PAINTED DIRECTLY ON TO THE SURFACE.

Fibre-reactive dyes (also known by their trade name of Procion®) work best on cotton or rayon fabrics. They won't work on synthetic fabrics. The colours are a little more muted on silk as the silk fibres do not absorb as much as cotton, but there are numerous silk dyes which can be fixed by steaming or ironing.

Fibre-reactive dyes need a fixative to make them fast. If this is used properly these dyes are reasonably light-fast and can be hand or machine-washed. This makes them ideal for dyeing garments.

Just like cooks, batik artists all have their favourite dye recipes so do not worry if you come across different ones. Here are two suggestions.

DIP-DYEING
You need a bowl or tray large enough to immerse the fabric, the dye powder, salt and soda ash. These quantities will dye 1 sq m of fine cotton in 1 litre cold water.

First make a salt solution by dissolving 60g salt in hot water and a soda solution of 10g soda ash in hot water. Keep these separate for the time being. The amount of dye powder you use will depend very much on how deep a colour you want – it could be anything from 2 – 5 grams. Again mix it to a smooth paste with warm water.

Add the dye paste and the salt solution to 1 litre cold water, stir and then add your cotton.

After about ten minutes, remove the cloth and add the soda solution and stir again before replacing the fabric. Leave for about another ten minutes. Remember to crack the wax wherever you want a crackle effect. If you don't want crackle, handle the fabric very carefully.

Take the fabric out and dry thoroughly (a humid atmosphere seems to work best). The dye process is still going on while drying so do not hurry it.

Once the fabric is thoroughly dry it can be washed.

HAND-PAINTING
Powdered dyes and their fixing solution should not be mixed together until you are ready to start dyeing. It's a good idea to make up a fix solution and keep it in a plastic bottle so that it is ready to use at any time.

Take 1 teaspoon urea, 1 teaspoon sodium bicarbonate and $\frac{1}{2}$ teaspoon soda ash.

Mix them with a little hot water and then add to 1.5 litres cold water.

Make up small amounts of dye in yoghurt pots. Add anything from a few grains to a whole teaspoon of dye to 2 tablespoons of fixing solution. Again the amount of dye powder you use depends very much on the depth of colour. These will be effective for 3 – 4 hours; so don't make up more than you need.

Keep your work on its frame for hand-painting. You can start by wetting the fabric, as this will encourage the dyes to bleed into each other. There are almost as many techniques for applying dye as there are for applying wax, so have fun and experiment.

Dye can be rubbed, sponged, painted, splashed, sprayed or dripped on to the fabric. Grains of rock salt or dry dye powder can be dropped on to the wet dyed fabric to give very interesting results. Blot off any excess dye from waxed areas and remember to dry the fabric thoroughly.

TEACHING CHILDREN TO BATIK

YOU SHOULD TAKE PARTICULAR CARE REGARDING HEALTH AND HAZARDS WHEN WORKING WITH CHILDREN.

- The room should be well ventilated, well lit and have enough working space, and flat surfaces for the number of children.

- There should be access to a water supply or sink.

- There should be a sufficient number of electrical power points. All leads should be safely positioned.

- Dyes should be pre-mixed in easy-to-use containers.

- The drying area should be organised and uncluttered.

- The children should be supervised when ironing out the wax.

- Waxpots have to be safe and easy to use. Thermostatically-controlled ones are the best. It is essential to warn the children of the hazards of working with hot wax.

- Surfaces and clothing need to be protected. It is advisable to use rubber gloves when working with dyes.

SOME WAX TECHNIQUES TO TRY WITH CHILDREN

■ Drip wax, do candle rubbings, draw a pattern or shapes in wax crayon or oil pastel on paper and paint over a dye colour. The waxed area will resist the dye.

■ Doodle with wax and write names and patterns on paper and fabric. Paint or dip in one dark colour.

■ Draw an outline of a bird in wax on paper and paint on different coloured dyes.

■ Use stamps or objects to apply the wax to create repeating patterns.

■ Wax a pattern using different sizes of brushes – preferably hog-hair and not man-made fibres.

■ Cut out a shape in sticky-back paper and place it on the fabric. Dip the brush in wax and spatter the wax by hitting the brush against a stick. Tell the children to take care that other work is moved out of the way in case the wax gets spattered elsewhere.

■ Draw and doodle with wax using a canting or kystka. Paint on different colours. When dry wax over the colours you want to keep and then dye the whole piece in a dark colour. The bright squiggles will stand out against the dark background.

■ Paint the fabric in different colours first. Dry and then block out areas in wax leaving a narrow space in between them, ie leaving a continuous space unwaxed around each shape. Dye the material in a dark colour and it should turn out like a stained glass – the dark areas being like lead lines.

■ Try the etching technique on page 33.

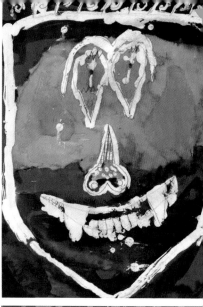

Love Song
Peter Wenger
Batik on cotton
115 x 170 cm

The Javanese definition of batik, "a point of light in the dark", was virtually at the beginning of my interest in art. It had such a powerful impact on my imagination that subsequently all my work derives directly from it. Throughout the years my work has been a continuous investigation into the aesthetic properties unique to resist-painting methods. This concern provides me with endless inspiration resulting in work which aims at representing the visual phenomena of resist-painting as clearly and concisely as possible in all their varied forms.

(photo: Art Van Go)

Aspect
Noel Dyrenforth
Batik on silk
54 x 54 cm

I've never been complacent about batik. I've constantly explored it for my own intuitive creative ends, methods, challenges, and concepts and vice versa... rules are broken, redefined... risks taken! In batik the molten wax hardens in the cloth resisting the promiscuous ebb of the dye. My make-up and motivation is symbolically echoed in this reaction between definitive and organic structure.

(photo: Art Van Go)

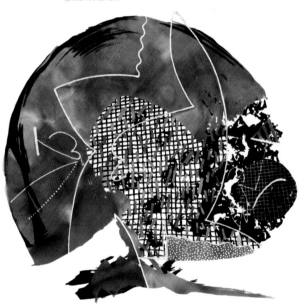

CONTEMPORARY BATIK

CONTEMPORARY BATIK IS MARKEDLY DIFFERENT FROM MORE TRADITIONAL AND FORMAL STYLES. ARTISTS CAN TAKE ADVANTAGE OF AN EVER WIDENING RANGE OF MATERIALS AND TECHNIQUES TO EXPLORE THIS UNIQUE PROCESS IN NEW AND EXCITING WAYS.

Although the craft of batik originates in traditional societies, the techniques of making it are continually developing in all kinds of exciting and different ways.

Using new techniques, new materials and new concepts contemporary batik challenges the usual perception of batik as a traditional craft. Once the possibilities are discovered, the flexibility of the batik process becomes apparent demonstrating the original effects achievable with wax and dye.

The contemporary work that follows has been chosen to present a wide variety of techniques, materials and forms of expression.

Sea Fret
Heather Gatt
Batik on cotton
77 x 57 cm

Light on water is a theme that excites and fascinates me, recurring in my work time and time again. I am in awe of the sea and living on the North Sea coast, I am fortunate to have the opportunity of observing its changing moods and hypnotic patterns, enjoying the challenge of translating these into batik. Working on fine cotton and drawing out my design with a 2B pencil, I use a selection of brushes and cantings to apply the wax resist. The fibre-reactive dyes are applied on to wet cloth or dry, using a soft brush, tissue or sponge.

(photo: Art Van Go)

Blue Bird
Alla Sviridenko
Batik on silk
90 x 90 cm

I am an artist from Belarus and use silk painting, print, batik, and tie-dye, often mixing different techniques together. *Blue Bird"* is an image with a lot of meaning for me. My name Alla means bird and my favourite colour is blue which signifies hope and safety. The woman with wings in the picture is like me taking care of my soul in my hands. I'm ready to fly at any time.

Portrait of Than Singh Bhoj
Jonathan Evans
Batik on cotton
56 x 77 cm

When I first went to live in Northern India, my paintings reflected the spectacular Himalayan landscape that surrounded me. But as time has passed I have focused much more on the tiny details of the life around me and in particular upon the people in my local village where every face seems to tell a story. Than Singh Bhoj is my nearest neighbour; an ex-soldier and chai-shop owner and very much of the Old School, he has been a close friend of mine for fifteen years. It was important to me to record him before he and his generation disappear for his lifestyle and values will soon vanish as India goes through tremendous changes.

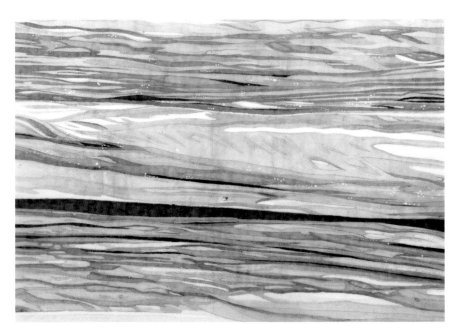

Snow
Andrea Trabitsch
Batik on rice paper
49 x 34 cm

"Snow" is one in a series of three batiks. I created it as I was trying to cope with my winter depression, which regularly sets in during the first snowfalls in November. At that time of the year, temperatures turn to freezing cold, driving conditions get bad and I have to bundle up to stay warm. By January, I have usually adapted to the low temperatures and even prefer the white and bluish colours of my surroundings and the clear and clean layers of snow on the landscape to the brown wasteland of mud.

(photo: L.Beck)

Mountain Landscape
Sheila Cook
Batik on cotton
38 x 38 cm

When working on *"Mountain Landscape"* I used the traditional canting and brush to apply wax to some parts of the design; additionally I used masking out and wax printing techniques using junk materials. These latter methods gave me the rugged impression which I wanted to achieve.

(photo: Art Van Go)

Rhoscolyn Rocks
Barbara Meynell
Batik on silk
71 x 52 cm

Inspired by colour and subtle transitions of light in nature, my technique involves painting on silk using Kniazeff dyes and wax as a resist. I draw many fine lines with the canting to recreate reflections of light in a landscape. Dyes are applied by brush in translucent layers finishing with a dip in the darkest dye. The inspiration for "**Rhoscolyn Rocks"** came from seeing beautiful coloured strata in Rhoscolyn Cove, Anglesey. In the afternoon sun they seemed to flow together in a unified, shimmering whole. Although there is no focal point the eye is taken into this intense moment of vision.

In Motion I
Elisa Quevedo
Batik on silk with embroidery and trapunto
50 x 40 cm

For me, batik is a ticket to a fascinating adventure, which makes you discover the immense possibilities of creating very personal images with a marbling effect. I work mostly on different qualities of silk and then create a 3D effect by applying machine stitching and trapunto on to my work. Movement is the inspiration for this piece: bubbles travelling from one place to the other, in a constant change of size, colour and shape.

(photo: Art Van Go)

Pier in Decay
Angela Lenman
Batik on paper
69 x 61 cm

The decaying splendour of the pier at Brighton was a perfect subject for a batik on paper, particularly for the amazing colours which bleach will give you. As a keen student of architecture, and particularly older, dilapidated buildings, the pier caught my imagination years ago, and for once, I actually did one of those things you think there's always time for, and booked on to a guided walk out on to the pier, already badly stricken following the hurricane. Now, of course, it is virtually gone. For me the batik evokes the haunting sadness of its once-grand halls and bustling walkways, nesting seagulls now its only visitors.

(photo: Art Van Go)

West Cork: Winter
Celia Weston
Batik on cotton
47 x 81 cm

I am intrigued by the interplay of shape and colour, by the possibility of a pure visual aesthetic that nevertheless remains accessible. I want to create work that generates a visceral excitement like the excitement I feel when I get to see my favourite abstracts. Sometimes an image with shape and colour is formed in my imagination and sometimes, as with this work, the external world is the inspiration. Here are the angularities and sharp colours of a sunny, strippe rural winter roadscape, portrayed in juxtapositions made possible by the challenging medium of batik.

(photo: Art Van Go)

Structures – London Eye
Diana Fenney
Batik on paper
44 x 59 cm

The white beams, the red power systems and the turquoise cabin roofs in bright sunshine made such an exciting pattern against the distant London scenes. The picture was very difficult and demanded careful planning and a steady hand! All the structures had to be completed with wax protecting them and then the distant landscape filled in afterwards. Working on paper gives a much greater control in containing the spread of the dyes than would be possible on cloth. The final wax is never removed completely and gives the colours great intensity.

In Other Words (detail)
Hélène de Ridder
Batik on cotton
Nine tubes 9 x 60 cm each

Although I am not a speaking word-painter, I love playing with words in my batik works. Letters and handwritings, words and thoughts are a beloved source of inspiration for me. Fifteen years ago somebody listened to my silent story. There was no sound, only written language. An exchange of words and thoughts. I started to enjoy writing. Writing what I thought. But nobody heard me. This was the origin, the sprouting of my written batiks.

Four Flowers
Helen Heery
Batik on paper
52 x 32 cm

My inspiration comes mainly from the spontaneity of the batik process, coupled with the stimuli of natural colours and forms. I use a wide variety of tools to apply the wax and dyes, which lead to an infinite number of abstract designs creating images with distinctly vibrant characteristics. "*Four Flowers*" reflects my many visits to tropical climates and my vivid, colourful garden in North London.

(photo: Art Van Go)

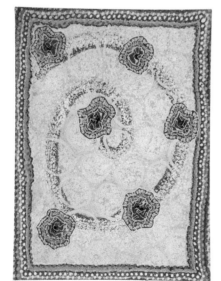

Swirl
Jane Christie
Batik on cotton
60 x 80 cm

This piece was inspired by cell structures as seen through a microscope.

(photo: Art Van Go)

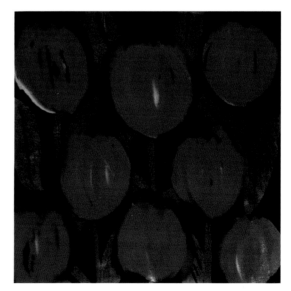

Red Tulips
Jenn Adamson
Batik on velvet
42 x 42 cm

This work was achieved by waxing and applying dye on the reverse side of the silk viscose velvet. As the two sides produce a very different effect, the work is sandwiched between two pieces of wood and can be shown on either side.

Drift
Dorothy Morris
Batik collage on cotton
91 x 30 cm each

"Drift" triptych was inspired by my journey from the coast of Ferryside to the coast of Pembrokeshire. I have also "drifted" from my secure teaching profession in Carmarthenshire, drawn by the rugged beauty of the Pembrokeshire coast where my studio is based. In these collaged batiks, I have tried to capture the geographic strata and patterns of the rocks and the waters around there. Beautiful, intense and dangerous, these waters may entice but they are also to be respected.

(photo: Art Van Go)

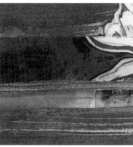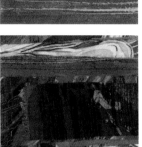

New Zealand Garden
Helen Dougall
Batik on cotton
92 x 50 cm

Most of my batiks are based on observational drawings or colour sketches. This is based on my cousin's garden in New Zealand, where I only had time for a minimal pastel sketch of the rather wild sloping garden looking down through a gate on to a pond with water-lily leaves. What struck me was the variety of trees and cacti that surrounded the garden where hens with their chicks ran free. Initially, I was not satisfied with the resulting batik composition, although it contained the elements I wanted. I cut the batik into strips and rearranged them, having worked out the juxtaposition, and then sewed them together. This produced an abstract version of the garden with all the textures, colours and patterns that had impressed me.

Kimono
Heather Koumi
Batik on cotton
76 x 76 cm

In this piece called "**Kimono**" I wanted to use different ways of applying wax in specific areas, within the constraints of shape and colour organisation. This is in direct contrast to my usual style of free brush marks, flowing colours and spontaneous wax application, loosely based on a design idea.

(photo: Art Van Go)

Vanity
Christa Corner
Batik on cotton
37 x 37 cm

When looking through a fashion magazine I saw a photograph of a model. It was her pose modelling jewellery and the way she held her head which attracted me and which provoked an impression of sheer "vanity". Apart from an outline, I didn't give the face any clearly defined features, preferring to leave it to the onlooker to complete the picture.

(photo: Art Van Go)

Ballet Dancer
Christine Nunn
Batik on silk
50 x 61 cm

I find batik on silk to be an exciting medium. Silk has an innate ability to capture light in the work as well as allowing the artist to work in fine detail. Here the ballet dancer is bathed in light illuminating the subject.

(photo: Art Van Go)

Freedom
Sipra Majumder
Batik on leather
23 x 38 cm

I graduated in graphic art but in addition was trained in India in batik on leatherwork and woodcarving. For batik I use textiles, leather and handmade paper. I often use hot wax, paste, glue and other media including powder leather dyes. This work was made using a paint-resisting paste through a complex technique.

(photo: Art Van Go)

Reclining Nude
Joan James
Batik on cotton
45 x 48 cm

I like to work from my original
drawings, translating them into
the technique of batik. I work
slowly, building up layers of
wax and dye. I constantly search
for new marks to create textures
with cantings, brushes or
unconventional tools. I then
strive to control and manipulate
the tools and textures to
produce an end result –
sometimes successfully,
very often not!.Fabric, dye,
wax and the human form
present a real challenge.

(photo: Art Van Go)

Eek!
Gail Thompson
Batik on cotton
80 x 147 cm

The ancient technique of batik
was chosen to create this picture
because of its tactile and sensuous
qualities. The wax is applied by
dripping and brushing. The dye
saturates deeply into the cloth,
creating vibrant and exciting colours,
which add resonance to the final
piece. "***Eek!***" was inspired by
nature's transient colours
and influenced by the dynamic
movement of Action Painting
of the '50s and '60s.

(photo: Art Van Go)

Divides
Jenifer Bess Sharpstone
Batik on paper
90 x 66 cm

Hot wax and cold dyes – it's the mix of unexpected media that excites me.
There is the element of the witches in Macbeth about batik… hubble bubble toil
and trouble… dash of urea, pinch of soda ash… just a little more blood red
powder. The feeling that I am in charge of the potions and the magic. The whole
picture changing with a dash of bleach, a slew of dye. And the wonderful pervading
smell of hot wax in my studio. Yes, definite elements of… hubble, bubble…

(photo: Art Van Go)

The Movement of Changing Season
Keijin Ihaya
Rozome on four silk scrolls
20 x 150 cm each

Nature gives me strong energy to live. When I express this feeling through rozome, creating patterns on cloth, I feel a sense of restraint. However, I always play with my imagination and unconsciously enjoy freedom within the limitations of the rozome technique.

Carnival
Ann Hyde-Harrison
Batik on cotton
61 x 51 cm

This piece records my memories of a visit to Trinidad when we borrowed a friend's house for the Carnival. The colours, costumes and music were fantastic. The batik was made on black cotton which was part bleached out.

(photo: Art Van Go)

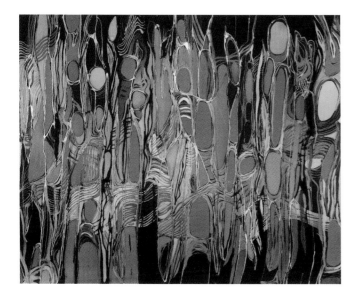

Grief
Rosi Robinson
Batik on cotton
69 x 55 cm

Travelling has been my predominant inspiration over the years.
The subject matter of my batik paintings is as diverse as Chinese
rooftops and English sporting scenes to abstract ripples in a pond.
"*Grief*" was originally created for an exhibition titled "Images
Speak a Thousand Words".
(photo: Art Van Go)

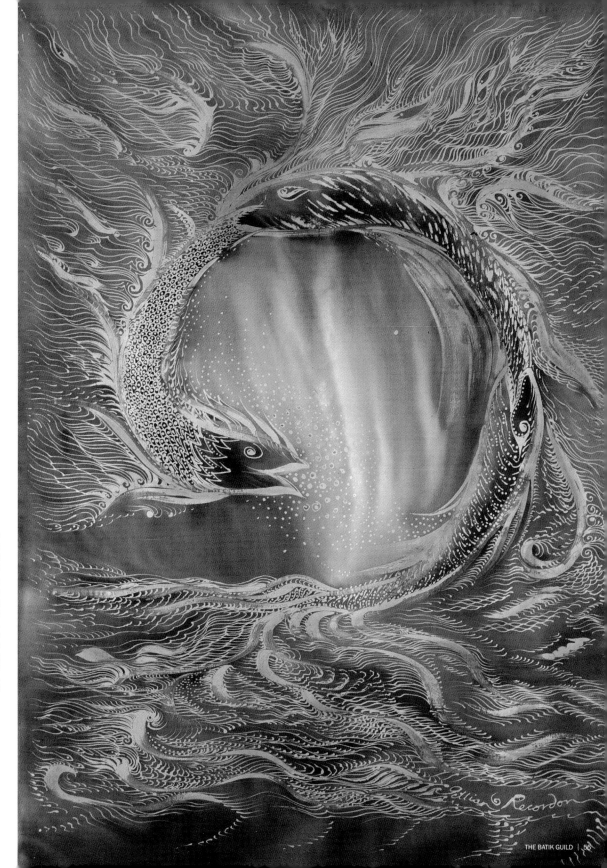

Fire and Ice
Gillian Recordon
Batik on silk
103 x 148 cm

This piece is a representation
of the mythical serpent of the
underworld, the Ouroboros, who
symbolises the perpetual cycle
of birth, death and completion.
The silk was pre-dyed with a
graded colour wash. The wax
resist was applied with a canting
and brush. It was then over-dyed
with brushes on to wet silk.

(photo: Reeve Photography)

The Palm House
Gill Curry
Batik on cotton
73 x 73 cm

This batik is based on The Palm House, Sefton Park, Liverpool, which was built in 1896 to house exotic plants and sculptures; it is a three-tiered octagonal structure of wrought and cast iron with 3,000 panes of glass. After extensive war damage a petition succeeded in obtaining a grant to restore the building and in September 2001 it was reopened. The batik celebrates this event.

The Letter
Kay Baxendall
Batik on paper
56 x 40 cm

I intended this painting to be a balance between figurative and abstract. It is held together by the predominating blue colour and the network of black lines, which define the forms. The final black dye penetrates the edges of the other dyes in a way typical of batik. I used a round Japanese brush.
(photo: Art Van Go)

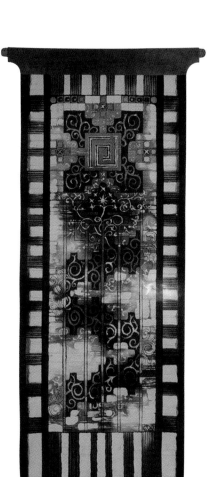

Trellis
Gwen Jackson
Batik on cotton
45 x 115 cm

I have been working in batik for over four decades. Current work is mostly small scale on silk; however, all have been hanging-cloths of silk, linen, or cotton of which "*Trellis*" is one of the smallest and most recent. Several are in private collections and two can be seen in the chapel of Holy Trinity Church in Exmouth, Devon.
(photo: S. Bartholomew)

Earth, Air, Darkness and Light
Jane Brunning
Batik on silk and cotton layers
80 x 110 cm

I enjoy expressing myself through the medium of batik, and am developing work that encourages the eye to travel through my pieces by using layers of fabric to be enjoyed as journeys. There are always time implications in the subject matter, whether in the lifespan of natural forms or the flow of weather systems. The journey taken depends entirely on the life as lived by the person viewing the work.

Adrift
Noel Dyrenforth
Batik on cotton
165 x 138 cm

My recurring theme is about
the cutting forces in society,
which intentionally confuse
and fragment, divide and
rule... to enslave the spirit.
Submission or chaos can
prevail unless the enduring
self-awareness can
transcend and readjust.
I am an optimist. I hope my
work gives a glimpse of how
vigilant we have to be to
protect our liberty.
(photo: Art Van Go)

Covered
Brigitte Willach
Batik on cotton
80 x 60 cm

"Covered" in this case is not only a description and title of my painting. It also describes more or less the batik technique. Hidden under
the snow the beauty and colourfulness appears after the melting snow. Is it not the same with the batik after the wax resist and dyeing?
Everything needs time, and a space to grow up and develop.

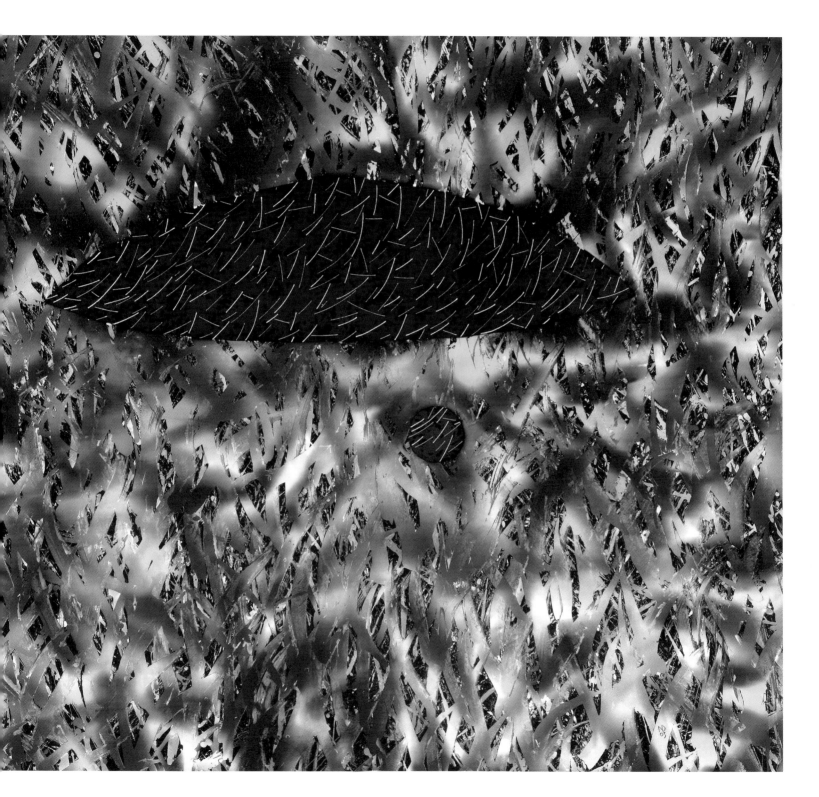

Lillian as Daphne
Marina Elphick
Batik on cotton satin
122 x 182 cm

"Lillian" was worked from life
and is a true portrait of a good
friend and creative spirit.

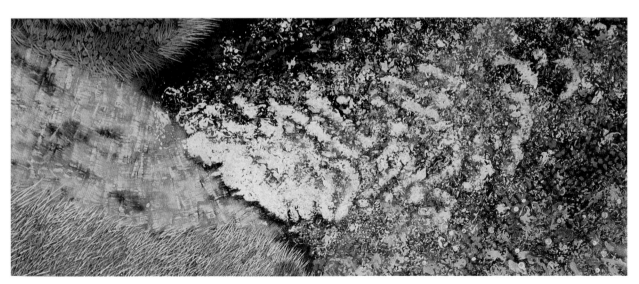

Nesting Coot
Anne Bologna
Batik on cotton
38 x 60 cm

The textures of fabric and paper and the
flexibility of the dyeing process make batik
an ideal medium on which to capture the
beauty of birds and their habitats. Each
picture is unique and the combinations of
images and techniques are unlimited. My
work is a reflection of the living landscape
and seascape of West Cork where I have
my studio.

Source of Penpont Water
Robin Paris
Batik on cotton
165 x 67 cm

Influenced by traditional Asian
and Cornish resourcefulness,
I adapt and create waxing tools
from scrap and found objects,
such as bicycle chainwheels.
Achieving textural effects
absolutely unobtainable with
conventional tools, they also
speed up the resist process
while maintaining that essential
union between artist and their
work. Water (especially rivers),
nature, culture and the
interconnectedness of things
are at the heart of my work.

Aix-en-Provence
Wendy Evans
Batik on cotton
61 x 74 cm

On a remarkable August visit to the
South of France I immersed myself in
Provençal art and culture, sketching
places and subjects previously painted
by artists from Cézanne's mountains
to Van Gogh's sunflowers. My mind
filled with artistic impressions I
explored the busy Old Town area of
beautiful Aix-en-Provence, when from
a cool dark café interior a girl emerged
into the glaring sunshine carrying a
huge vase of sunflowers. She set the
intensely coloured display on a little
café table covered in a brightly
patterned cloth. This image stayed
with me and became the inspiration for
my painterly batik "*Aix-en-Provence*"
which is part of a body of work
produced as a result of my visit.
(photo: Art Van Go)

Loch Sunart
Anne Dye
Batik on cotton
43 x 43 cm

I am greatly influenced by the scenery of the Scottish Highlands, where I live. I drive along Loch Sunart every day and in this simple piece tried to capture its mood on a rather misty, still day. I started out with a wash using several dyes but once I had waxed the sky and water, leaving gaps for the birds and landmass, I worked straightforwardly from light to dark.

(photo: Art Van Go)

USEFUL CONTACTS

Art Van Go
Suppliers of fine art and textile materials from their gallery or travelling van.
Tel: 01438 814946
www.artvango.co.uk

Batik in Brighton
Classes in batik.
adamson36a@yahoo.co.uk

Batik in Cornwall
Batik workshops, retreats, talks and lectures.
www.robinparis.co.uk

Batik in Schools
Batik for children and teachers.
www.batikinschools.co.uk

Colourcraft
Specialise in the manufacture and supply of high quality dyes and auxiliary chemicals with full technical backup for all products.
Tel: 0114 242 1431
www.colourcraftltd.com

Craftynotions.com
Provide a wide variety of media and materials for anyone with a passion for textiles.
Tel: 01636 700862
www.craftynotions.com

Fibrecrafts
A full range of equipment for batikers including tools, dyes, waxes.
Tel: 01483 565800
www.fibrecrafts.com

Rainbow Silks
Supplies for silk painting, textile and paper art, embroidery and more!
Tel: 01494 862111
www.rainbowsilks.co.uk

Simplee Silk
Demonstrations, workshops and talks on batik, shibori techniques and silk painting.
cnlc1@cam.ac.uk

Textile Techniques
A full range of batik equipment plus Javanese batik and other hand-made textiles from around the world. Talks and Workshops.
Tel: 01588 638712
www.textiletechniques.co.uk

The Batik Guild
www.batikguild.org.uk

Whaleys (Bradford) Ltd
Suppliers of all types of fabrics, many of which are prepared for dyeing, printing and batik work.
Tel: 01274 576718
www.whaleys-bradford.ltd.uk

PLACES TO SEE BATIK IN THE UK

The British Museum
Great Russell Street
London WC1B 3DG
Tel: 020 7323 8299
www.thebritishmuseum.ac.uk

Batik from Indonesia, the rest of Asia and Africa, although some were probably produced in England for the African market. There are also some earlier batiks including those collected by Sir Stamford Raffles.

Fitzwilliam Museum
Trumpington Street
Cambridge CB2 1RB
Tel: 01223 332900
www.fitzmuseum.cam.ac.uk

Examples of resist dyed textiles from Japan and Central Asia.

Glasgow Museums World Cultures
Museums Resource Centre
200 Woodhead Road
Glasgow G53 7NN
Tel: 0141 276 9317

The museums resource centre has a record of a book of batik specimens and a selection of Indian batik print and wax clothes.

Leeds Museum Resource Centre
Moorfield Road
Yeadon
Leeds LS19 7BN
Tel: 0113 214 6526

**University of Leeds
International Textiles Archive**
St Wilfred's Chapel
Moorland Road
Leeds LS2 9JT
Tel: 0113 343 3919
www.leedsmuseumscollections.co.uk

A small collection of batik from South-East Asia and a good representation of African resist-dyed fabrics.

Manchester Museum of Science & Industry
Liverpool Road
Castlefield
Manchester M3 4FP
Tel: 0161 832 2244
www.msim.org.uk

Collection of textile samples from the Paterson Zochonis Company, which traded extensively with West Africa in the 1960s, many have the Registered Designs paper attached to them.

Pitt Rivers Museum
South Parks Road
Oxford OX1 3PP
Tel: 01865 270927
www.prm.ox.ac.uk

This collection contains approximately 150 batik textiles at the Pitt Rivers Museum, mostly from South-East Asia and China.

Horniman Museum
100 London Road
Forest Hill
London SE23 3PQ
Tel: 020 8699 1872
www.horniman.ac.uk

Textiles from around the world in the museum's World Cultures (ethnography) collection.

South-East Asia Museum
Centre for South-East Asian Studies,
University of Hull
Cottingham Road
Hull HU6 7RX
www.hull.ac.uk/seas/study_facilities.html

The University's South-East Asian Museum possesses large collections of artefacts relating to the region, including textiles. There is also a permanent display of batik cloths from Sumatra.

National Museums of Scotland
Chambers Street
Edinburgh EH1 1JF
Tel: 0131 247 4219
www.nms.ac.uk

A significant number of batik items – the majority are Javanese; the African items are predominantly fabrics printed to resemble batik. There are also items relating to batik dyeing, such as stamps and some samples illustrating the process of dyeing.

Victoria & Albert Museum
Cromwell Road
South Kensington
London SW7 2RL
Tel: 020 742 2322 / 2323 / 2334
www.vam.ac.uk

The V&A holds an extensive collection of Javanese batik in the Indian and South-East Asia department study collection.

World Museum Liverpool
William Brown Street
Liverpool L3 8EN
Tel: 0151 478 4399
www.liverpoolmuseums.org.uk/wml

Asian collections with some excellent examples from Indonesia (including batik making equipment). Approximately 150 batik pieces from Java, including cloth, tools, dye samples and other utensils, mostly from the 1987 Gaffney collection.

SELECTED BOOKS AND WEBSITES

TRADITIONAL BATIK AND RELATED TEXTILES

Traditional African Textiles
John Gillow
Thames and Hudson

The Art of African Textiles
Duncan Clarke
Grange Books

African Textiles
Colour and Creativity Across a Continent
John Gillow
Thames and Hudson

Miao textiles
Gina Corrigan
Fabric Folios, British Museum Press

Miao Embroidery from South-West China:
Textiles from the Gina Corrigan Collection
Ruth Smith
Occidor Ltd.

Guizhou Province: Costume and Culture in Remote China
Gina Corrigan
Odyssey Guides

Batik – Design, Style & History
Fiona Kerlogue
Thames and Hudson

Traditional Indonesian Textiles
John Gillow
Thames and Hudson

Batik: from the Courts of Java and Sumatra
Rudolf G. Smend Collection
Rudolf G. Smend et al
Periplus Editions/Berkeley Books Pte Ltd

Sari to Sarong: Five Hundred Years of Indian and Indonesian Textile Exchange
Robyn Maxwell
National Gallery of Australia

Textiles of Southeast Asia: Tradition, Trade and Transformation
Robyn Maxwell
Periplus Editions/Berkeley Books Pte Ltd

The World of Rozome
Wax Resist Textiles of Japan
Betsy Sterling Benjamin
Kodansha Europe

CONTEMPORARY BATIK

Batik: Modern Concepts and Techniques
Noel Dyrenforth
B.T. Batsford Ltd

Batik
Sarah Tucker
The Crowood Press Ltd

Creative Batik
Rosi Robinson
Search Press Ltd

Silk painting: techniques and ideas
Jill Kennedy and Jane Varrall
B.T. Batsford Ltd

The Art Of Batik
The Batik Guild
www.batikguild.org.uk

DVD Useable and Wearable Batik,
Lee Creswell and Anne Dye
e-mail: cnlc1@cam.ac.uk

SELECTED WEBSITES

www.batikguild.org.uk
A gallery of members work, history, news, teachers, exhibitions, courses etc.

www.24hourmuseum.co.uk
24 Hour Museum is the UK's official guide to over 3,000 museums, galleries, exhibitions and heritage attractions.

www.craftscouncil.org.uk
The Crafts Council is the UK's national organisation for the promotion of contemporary crafts.

www.textilemuseum.org
Online access to the Textile Museum. As a museum, it is committed to its role as a centre of excellence in the scholarly research, conservation, interpretation and exhibition of textiles, with particular concern for the artistic, technical and cultural significance of its collections.

www.a2a.org.uk
A2A database contains catalogues of archives held across England and dating from the 1990s to the present day including an introduction to the origins and techniques of Indonesian batik.

www.adireafricantextiles.com
Information on all kinds of African textiles particularly adire.

www.abcwax.co.uk
The last manufacturer left in the UK of genuine West African waxprint.

www.expat.or.id/info/batik.html
General information on Indonesia with a good section on its textiles.

www.china.org.cn/e-groups
Information on all China's ethnic minority groups including their textiles.

www.smend.de
Rudolf Smend's Gallery in Cologne, Germany.